P9-BII-987

THE **W** ORD ON

THE NEW TESTAMENT

MIKE DeVRIES

JIM BURNS, GENERAL EDITOR

THE NATIONAL INSTITUTE OF YOUTH MINISTRY

Gospel Light

Gospel Light is an evangelical Christian publisher dedicated to serving the local church. We believe God's vision for Gospel Light is to provide church leaders with biblical, user-friendly materials that will help them evangelize, disciple and minister to children, youth and families.

We hope this Gospel Light resource will help you discover biblical truth for your own life and help you minister to youth. God bless you in your work.

For a free catalog of resources from Gospel Light please contact your Christian supplier or call 1-800-4-GOSPEL.

PUBLISHING STAFF

William T. Greig, Publisher

Dr. Elmer L. Towns, Senior Consulting Publisher

Dr. Gary S. Greig, Senior Consulting Editor

Jean Daly, Managing Editor

Pam Weston, Editorial Assistant

Kyle Duncan, Associate Publisher

Bayard Taylor, M.Div., Editor, Theological and Biblical Issues

Debi Thayer, Designer

ISBN 0-8307-1725-0
© 1996 by Jim Burns
All rights reserved.
Printed in U.S.A.

All Scripture quotations, unless otherwise indicated, are taken from the *Holy Bible, New International Version®. NIV®.* Copyright © 1973, 1978, 1984 by International Bible Society. Used by permission of Zondervan Publishing House. All rights reserved.
Other version used is:
The Message—The New Testament in Contemporary English by Eugene H. Peterson. © 1994 by NavPress. All rights reserved.

HOW TO MAKE CLEAN COPIES FROM THIS BOOK

YOU MAY MAKE COPIES OF PORTIONS OF THIS BOOK WITH A CLEAN CONSCIENCE IF:

• you (or someone in your organization) are the original purchaser;
• you are using the copies you make for a noncommercial purpose (such as teaching or promoting your ministry) within your church or organization;
• you follow the instructions provided in this book.

HOWEVER, IT IS ILLEGAL FOR YOU TO MAKE COPIES IF:

• you are using the material to promote, advertise or sell a product or service other than for ministry fund-raising;
• you are using the material in or on a product for sale;
• you or your organization are **not** the original purchaser of this book.

By following these guidelines you help us keep our products affordable.
Thank you,
Gospel Light

Permission to make photocopies or to reproduce by any other mechanical or electronic means in whole or in part of any designated* page, illustration or activity in this book is granted only to the original purchaser and is intended for noncommercial use within a church or other Christian organization. None of the material in this book may be reproduced for any commercial promotion, advertising or sale of a product or service. Sharing of the material in this book with other churches or organizations not owned or controlled by the original purchaser is also prohibited. All rights reserved.

*Pages with the following notation can be legally reproduced:

© 1996 by Gospel Light. Permission to photocopy granted.

PRAISE FOR YOUTHBUILDERS

Jim Burns knows young people. He also knows how to communicate to them. This study should be in the hands of every youth leader interested in discipling young people.

David Adams, Vice President, Lexington Baptist College

I deeply respect and appreciate the groundwork Jim Burns has prepared for true teenage discernment. *YouthBuilders* is timeless in the sense that the framework has made it possible to plug into any society, at any point in time, and to proceed to discuss, experience and arrive at sincere moral and Christian conclusions that will lead to growth and life changes. Reaching young people may be more difficult today than ever before, but God's grace is alive and well in Jim Burns and this wonderful curriculum.

Fr. Angelo J. Artemas, Youth Ministry Director, Greek Orthodox Archdiocese of North and South America

I heartily recommend Jim Burns's *YouthBuilders Group Bible Studies* because they are leader-friendly tools that are ready to use in youth groups and Sunday School classes. Jim addresses the tough questions that students are genuinely facing every day and, through his engaging style, challenges young people to make their own decisions to move from their current opinions to God's convictions taught in the Bible. Every youth group will benefit from this excellent curriculum.

Paul Borthwick, Minister of Missions, Grace Chapel

Jim Burns recognizes the fact that small groups are where life change happens. In this study he has captured the essence of that value. Further, Jim has given much thought to shaping this very effective material into a usable tool that serves the parent, leader and student.

Bo Boshers, Executive Director, Student Impact, Willow Creek Community Church

It is about time that someone who knows kids, understands kids and works with kids writes youth curriculum that youth workers, both volunteer and professional, can use. Jim Burns's *YouthBuilders Group Bible Studies* is the curriculum that youth ministry has been waiting a long time for.

Ridge Burns, President,
The Center for Student Missions

Jim Burns has done it again. He speaks to kids right where they are and helps them to understand what Christianity is about in their own terms.

Tony Campolo, Professor, Eastern College

There are very few people in the world who know how to communicate life-changing truth effectively to teens. Jim Burns is one of the best. *YouthBuilders Group Bible Studies* puts handles on those skills and makes them available to everyone. These studies are biblically sound, hands-on practical and just plain fun. This one gets a five-star endorsement—which isn't bad since there are only four stars to start with.

Ken Davis, President, Dynamic Communications

I don't know anyone who knows and understands the needs of the youth worker like Jim Burns. His new curriculum not only reveals his knowledge of youth ministry but also his depth and sensitivity to the Scriptures. *YouthBuilders Group Bible Studies* is solid, easy to use and gets students out of their seats and into the Word. I've been waiting for something like this for a long time!

Doug Fields, Pastor of High School, Saddleback Valley Community Church

Jim Burns has a way of being creative without being "hokey." *YouthBuilders Group Bible Studies* takes the age-old model of curriculum and gives it a new look with tools such as the Bible *Tuck-In*™ and Parent Page. Give this new resource a try and you'll see that Jim shoots straightforward on tough issues. The *YouthBuilders* series is great for leading small-group discussions as well as teaching a large class of junior high or high school students. The Parent Page will help you get support from your parents in that they will understand the topics you are dealing with in your group. Put Jim's years of experience to work for you by equipping yourself with this quality material.

Curt Gibson, Pastor to Junior High, First Church of the Nazarene of Pasadena

Once again, Jim Burns has managed to handle very timely issues with just the right touch. His *YouthBuilders Group Bible Studies* succeeds in teaching solid biblical values without being stuffy or preachy. The format is user-friendly, designed to stimulate high involvement and deep discussion. Especially impressive is the Parent Page, a long overdue tool to help parents become part of the Christian education loop. I look forward to using it with my kids!

David M. Hughes, Pastor, First Baptist Church, Winston-Salem

What do you get when you combine a deep love for teens, over 20 years' experience in youth ministry and an excellent writer? You get Jim Burns's *YouthBuilders* series! This stuff has absolutely hit the nail on the head. Quality Sunday School and small-group material is tough to come by these days, but Jim has put every ounce of creativity he has into these books.

Greg Johnson, author of
Getting Ready for the Guy/Girl Thing and
Keeping Your Cool While Sharing Your Faith

Jim Burns has a gift, the gift of combining the relational and theological dynamics of our faith in a graceful, relevant and easy-to-chew-and-swallow way. *YouthBuilders Group Bible Studies* is a hit, not only for teens but for teachers.

Gregg Johnson, National Youth Director,
International Church of the Foursquare Gospel

The practicing youth worker always needs more ammunition. Here is a whole book full of practical, usable resources for those facing kids face-to-face. *YouthBuilders Group Bible Studies* will get that blank stare off the faces of kids in your youth meeting!

Jay Kesler, President, Taylor University

I couldn't be more excited about the *YouthBuilders Group Bible Studies*. It couldn't have arrived at a more needed time. Spiritually we approach the future engaged in war with young people taking direct hits from the devil. This series will practically help teens who feel partially equipped to "put on the whole armor of God."

Mike MacIntosh, Pastor,
Horizon Christian Fellowship

In *YouthBuilders Group Bible Studies*, Jim Burns pulls together the key ingredients for an effective curriculum series. Jim captures the combination of teen involvement and a solid biblical perspective, with topics that are relevant and straightforward. This series will be a valuable tool in the local church.

Dennis "Tiger" McLuen, Executive Director,
Youth Leadership

My ministry takes me to the lost kids in our nation's cities where youth games and activities are often irrelevant and plain Bible knowledge for the sake of learning is unattractive. Young people need the information necessary to make wise decisions related to everyday problems. *YouthBuilders* will help many young people integrate their faith into everyday life, which after all is our goal as youth workers.

Miles McPherson, President, Project Intercept

Jim Burns's passion for teens, youth workers and parents of teens is evident in the *YouthBuilders Group Bible Studies*. He has a gift of presenting biblical truths on a level teens will fully understand, and youth workers and parents can easily communicate.

Al Menconi, President, Al Menconi Ministries

Youth ministry curriculum is often directed to only one spoke of the wheel of youth ministry—the adolescent. Not so with this material! Jim has enlarged the education circle, including information for the adolescent, the parent and the youth worker. *YouthBuilders Group Bible Studies* is youth and family ministry-oriented material at its best.

Helen Musick, Instructor of Youth Ministry, Asbury Seminary

Finally, a Bible study that has it all! It's action-packed, practical and biblical; but that's only the beginning. *YouthBuilders* involves students in the Scriptures. It's relational, interactive and leads kids toward lifestyle changes. The unique aspect is a page for parents, something that's usually missing from adolescent curriculum. Jim Burns has outdone himself. This isn't a home run—it's a grand slam!

Dr. David Olshine, Director of Youth Ministries, Columbia International University

Here is a thoughtful and relevant curriculum designed to meet the needs of youth workers, parents and students. It's creative, interactive and biblical—and with Jim Burns's name on it, you know you're getting a quality resource.

Laurie Polich, Youth Director, First Presbyterian Church of Berkeley

In 10 years of youth ministry I've never used a curriculum because I've never found anything that actively involves students in the learning process, speaks to young people where they are and challenges them with biblical truth—I'll use this! *YouthBuilders Group Bible Studies* is a complete curriculum that is helpful to parents, youth leaders and, most importantly, today's youth.

Glenn Schroeder, Youth and Young Adult Ministries, Vineyard Christian Fellowship, Anaheim

This new material by Jim Burns represents a vitality in curriculum and, I believe, a more mature and faithful direction. *YouthBuilders Group Bible Studies* challenges youth by teaching them how to make decisions rather than telling them what decisions to make. Each session offers teaching concepts, presents options and asks for a decision. I believe it's healthy, the way Christ taught and represents the abilities, personhood and faithfulness of youth. I give it an *A+*!

J. David Stone, President, Stone & Associates

Jim Burns has done it again! This is a practical, timely and reality-based resource for equipping teens to live life in the fast-paced, pressure-packed adolescent world of the '90s. A very refreshing creative oasis in the curriculum desert!

Rich Van Pelt, President, Alongside Ministries

YouthBuilders Group Bible Studies is a tremendous new set of resources for reaching students. Jim has his finger on the pulse of youth today. He understands their mind-sets, and has prepared these studies in a way that will capture their attention and lead to greater maturity in Christ. I heartily recommend these studies.

Rick Warren, Senior Pastor,
Saddleback Valley Community Church

CONTENTS

THANKS AND THANKS AGAIN!

First and foremost, thank-you to Jamie, my wife, and Joshua, my son. Words could never express what you mean to me. To my parents Lou and Judy DeVries and all of my family: Your love and support for me is incredible!!!

To Jim Burns: I thank God for our friendship and your encouragement in my life. I value our time together. Thanks for always being there.

To Jean Daly and everyone at Gospel Light: Thanks for your belief in me, this project, this series and youth ministry.

To our High School Ministry Assistants Jon Irving and Kim Klein; our intern Jill Willis, and my secretary Julie Jackman: I count it a privilege to not only call you my coworkers, but also my friends—I love you! You are the greatest and most gifted team I could ever ask for. Thanks for the sacrifice to see this dream become a reality! To Matt Wenger: thanks for all you mean to us; God has some incredible plans for you.

To the High School Ministries Team at Yorba Linda Friends Church: Joby and Sandy Anderson, Brian Arendt, Shana Beatty, Tracy Comer, Jill Fancher, Matt Given, Jay Hoff, Craig and Megan Jones, Bryl Lumby, Mike and Carol McMillan, Brian Novakoff, Sonia O'Bryan, Bob and Cecilia Ornelas, John Prevost, Julie Ronk, Heather Shook, Mary Kay Stephens, Steve Tingwall, Skip and Debi Wandrey, Melanie Washburn, Katrina White and Sophie Yu. You all mean the world to me. I thank God that He has allowed me to work as a part of our team with you all! Thank-you to all the high school students at "The EDGE" High School Ministries for your love, encouragement and allowing me to be your pastor.

To Pastor John Werhas: your belief in me has been more of an encouragement than you will ever know. To the rest of the staff of Yorba Linda Friends Church: I am blessed to be a part of our team.

To my Tuesday morning Bible Study: Thanks for your prayers and support. To Don Collins: you are truly "a friend that sticks closer than a brother." Love you, brother.

DEDICATION

To Jamie, my wife: I could never do what I do without you. I could never imagine being married to a more wonderful woman. I love you so very much—now and forever!!! You are such a gift from God and I am the most blessed man on earth.

To Joshua, my son: Ever since you came into my life, I've experienced the incredible love of God in a new way. You are a gift, a treasure, a priceless wonder. I love you so very much and I'm proud to be your Daddy! I love you always! I look forward to all that life has in store for us.

YOUTHBUILDERS GROUP BIBLE STUDIES

It's Relational—Students learn best when they talk, not when you talk. There is always a get-acquainted section in the Warm Up. All the experiences are based on building community in your group.

It's Biblical—With no apologies, this series is unashamedly Christian. Every session has a practical, relevant Bible study.

It's Experiential—Studies show that young people retain up to 85 percent of the material when they are *involved* in action-oriented, experiential learning. The sessions use role-plays, discussion starters, case studies, graphs and other experiential, educational methods. *We believe it's a sin to bore a young person with the gospel.*

It's Interactive—This study is geared to get students feeling comfortable with sharing ideas and interacting with peers and leaders.

It's Easy to Follow—The sessions have been prepared by Jim Burns to allow the leader to pick up the material and use it. There is little preparation time on your part. Jim did the work for you.

It's Adaptable—You can pick and choose from several topics or go straight through the material as a whole study.

It's Age Appropriate—In the "Team Effort" section, one group experience relates best to junior high students while the other works better with high school students. Look at both to determine which option is best for your group.

It's Parent Oriented—The Parent Page helps you to do youth ministry at its finest. Christian education should take place in the home as well as in the church. The Parent Page is your chance to come alongside the parents and help them have a good discussion with their kids.

It's Proven—This material was not written by someone in an ivory tower. It was written for young people and has already been used with them. They love it.

HOW TO USE THIS STUDY

The 12 sessions are divided into three stand-alone units. Each unit has four sessions. You may choose to teach all 12 sessions consecutively. Or you may use only one unit. Or you may present individual sessions. You know your best so you choose.

Each of the 12 sessions is divided into five sections.

Warm Up—Young people will stay in your youth group if they feel comfortable and make friends in the group. This section is designed for you and the students to get to know each other better. These activities are filled with history-giving and affirming questions and experiences.

Team Effort—Following the model of Jesus, the Master Teacher, these activities engage young people in the session. Stories, group situations, surveys and more bring the session to the students. There is an option for junior high/middle school students and one for high school students.

In the Word—Most young people are biblically illiterate. These Bible studies present the Word of God and encourage students to see the relevance of the Scriptures to their lives.

Things to Think About—Young people need the opportunity to really think through the issues at hand. These discussion starters get students talking about the subject and interacting on important issues.

Parent Page—A youth worker can only do so much. Reproduce this page and get it into the hands of parents. This tool allows quality parent/teen communication that really brings the session home.

The Bible Tuck-In™

It's a tear-out sheet you fold and place in your Bible, containing the essentials you'll need for teaching your group.

HERE'S HOW TO USE IT:

To prepare for the session, first study the session. Tear out the Bible *Tuck-In*™ and personalize it by making notes. Fold the Bible *Tuck-In*™ in half on the dotted line. Slip it into your Bible for easy reference throughout the session. The Key Verse, Biblical Basis and Big Idea at the beginning of the Bible *Tuck-In*™ will help you keep the session on track. With the Bible *Tuck-In*™ your students will see that your teaching comes from the Bible and won't be distracted by a leader's guide.

HEROES OF THE NEW TESTAMENT

LEADER'S PEP TALK

Everyone needs a hero. Yet as we look around our world today, where are the heroes? Are they on the television, in the movies or on the radio? What does it take to be a hero? In a lost and searching world, our students need to see and meet real-life heroes.

As I look in the Scriptures, I keep feeling myself drawn to the heroes. Peter, Paul, Timothy, Mary and scores of others have one thing in common. What makes them heroes is not that they were giants of the faith. It wasn't that they were perfect or had it all together. What makes them heroes is that they were real, and their love for God was real. They were real-life people with real-life struggles, yet they had an extraordinary love for God.

If there is something that our students need, it's real-life heroes. They need to see that heroes are real people with real problems but with an incredible love for God. The pages of the Scriptures are filled with heroes. Heroes who stood for what was right—what was godly. Heroes who had an intense love for God. In addition to the heroes of the New Testament, there stand other heroes, ones that will never be in the pages of the Scriptures, yet I believe they are heroes in the eyes of the One who matters most. I believe that one of those heroes is you. Your students may never tell you this, but believe me, you are a hero. So to all of you who are real with students, who love them unconditionally, who choose to be transparent with your life, who love God and are willing to share that love relationship with young people, you are today's hero. When it comes time to be with Him in heaven, I believe if any hero will get the applause of the saints and angels, it will be you because you are a hero in your work for His kingdom.

PETER:
FAILURE IS NEVER FINAL

KEY VERSE

"But he said to me, 'My grace is sufficient for you, for my power is made perfect in weakness.'"
2 Corinthians 12:9

BIBLICAL BASIS

Matthew 14:25-31;
Mark 14:27-31,66-72; 16:6,7;
John 1:35-42; 21:15-19;
Acts 2:14,22-24,36-41; 3:1-8;
2 Corinthians 12:9,10

THE BIG IDEA

Even when you feel like a failure, God is ready and willing to give you a second chance and use you to help fulfill His plans for the Kingdom.

AIMS OF THIS SESSION

During this session you will guide students to:
• Examine the life of Peter;
• Discover that God can use us in the midst of our weaknesses and failures;
• Implement a newfound hope in response to the faithfulness of God.

WARM UP

THE THRILL OF VICTORY AND THE AGONY OF DEFEAT—

Students discuss their personal reactions to victory and defeat.

TEAM EFFORT— JUNIOR HIGH/ MIDDLE SCHOOL

FAILURE IS NEVER FINAL: TWO PORTRAITS—

Abraham Lincoln and Thomas Edison experienced countless failures and didn't give up!

TEAM EFFORT— HIGH SCHOOL

PETER, THIS IS YOUR LIFE!—

Students role-play scenes from the life of Peter.

IN THE WORD

PETER: FROM FAILURE TO FOLLOWER—

A Bible study on how God transformed Peter from a failure to a leader.

THINGS TO THINK ABOUT (OPTIONAL)

Questions to get students thinking and talking about how to see past their own weaknesses and failures to the potential within them to serve God in His power.

PARENT PAGE

A tool to get the session into the home and allow parents and young people to discuss the purpose of failure in our lives.

PETER:
FAILURE IS
NEVER FINAL

LEADER'S DEVOTIONAL

"'Lord, if it is you,' Peter replied, 'tell me to come to you on the water.' 'Come,' he said. Then Peter got down out of the boat, walked on the water and came toward Jesus" (Matthew 14:28,29).

Jesus' schedule for the day would be familiar to youth workers. After teaching all day, Jesus proceeded to feed His hungry flock and send them home. He dismissed the disciples before He retreated to be alone with God. Personally, I would have opted for a nap, or a nice quiet walk along the shore of the Galilean Sea. Jesus chose to be with the Father. Such a picture portrays the nature of Jesus Christ and unveils His motive for His mission on earth.

In the meantime, the disciples found themselves in rough waters. By the time Jesus cruised onto the scene, the fishermen feared the elements, the political zealots wished they were lobbying on dry land and the others wanted to be anywhere else, even if it meant collecting taxes.

Jesus immediately noticed the fear of His men. He said, "Take courage. It is I. Don't be afraid" (Matthew 14:27). God will reveal Himself when we're afraid. When you face fear, frustration and futility, replace your discouragement—your "dis-courage" with the courage offered by Christ.

Peter tried to do just that. Fast forward a few frames in the story: Peter's courage is fleeting. He doubts. He sinks. He fails. Do you ever feel more fear than faith, more waves than wonder? Does your work with people seem blown away by the wind? Learn from our friend Peter whom Jesus labeled "The Rock" ("Rocky" if he were alive today).

When you find yourself in the lifeboat buffeted by the elements, follow Peter's lead. First, pray to Jesus "Tell me to come to you." Second, listen (and wait!) for God's invitation "Come." Don't jump overboard with your own best intentions. Sometimes failure is the result of our premature departures. Thirdly, leave behind everything you know and trust—your confidence in your career, the comfort of the boat, the company of your friends and go to Christ. Finally, get out and walk with Jesus. After all is said and done, prayed and planned, do what you've got to do. Life is a voyage, not a safe harbor.

What happened? Peter took the step of faith, but then he took his eyes off Jesus and sank. He nearly drowned. He failed. Then he found himself face-to-face with the living God admonishing him "You of little faith, why did you doubt?" Peter's failure led him to a deeper faith and a powerful future. With Peter and the rest of us failure is never final. Bon voyage! (Written by Doug Webster)

**"Courage is resistance to fear and mastery of fear, not absence of it."
—Mark Twain**

PETER:
FAILURE IS NEVER FINAL

K EY VERSE

"But he said to me, 'My grace is sufficient for you, for my power is made perfect in weakness.'"
2 Corinthians 12:9

B IBLICAL BASIS

Matthew 14:25-31; Mark 14:27-31,66-72; 16:6,7; John 1:35-42; 21:15-19; Acts 2:14,22-24,36-41; 3:1-8; 2 Corinthians 12:9,10

T HE BIG IDEA

Even when you feel like a failure, God is ready and willing to give you a second chance and use you to help fulfill His plans for the Kingdom.

W ARM UP (5-10 MINUTES)

THE THRILL OF VICTORY AND THE AGONY OF DEFEAT

• Go to your local video store and browse around for videos depicting victory and defeat. They could be sports videos or motion pictures that vividly portray "the thrill of victory and the agony of defeat." Great videos to use include: *Karate Kid* (the final tournament scene), one of the *Rocky* films (any of the final fight scenes), *The Natural* (when Robert Redford's character hits the home run to win the game), or any of the *Sports Yearbook* videos.

• Show short "victory" and "defeat" clips from the selected videos.

After viewing the clips, discuss the following questions with the whole group or in small groups of three or four:

1. How do you think it might have felt to be one of the victorious characters shown in the videos?

— Fold —

What were the results of Peter's obedience?

2. Even though Peter felt like a failure, God used him as a part of His plan to touch lives. What hope can be found for you personally from these verses in Acts?

....

SO WHAT?

1. After looking at the four scenes, in what way can you relate to Peter?

....

2. What are some of your failures and weaknesses that you need to give over to God?

....

3. What are some of the areas of your life in which you desperately need to sense the restoration of God?

....

4. In what areas does God want to use you?

....

5. What are two things that you learned from this session?

....

What action step will you take to apply what you have learned about yourself?

....

T HINGS TO THINK ABOUT (OPTIONAL)

• Use the questions on page 25 after or as a part of "In the Word."
1. Why is it so difficult to see past our weaknesses and failures to the potential God sees in us?

2. How does it feel to know that...
   God knows your potential?
   God knows your weaknesses and failures?
   God is in the business of restoration?
   God wants to use you?

3. How does 2 Corinthians 12:9,10 relate to your life and this session?

P ARENT PAGE

• Distribute page to parents.

2. How do you think it might have felt to be one of the defeated characters?

3. If you could script your own movie scene with yourself as the star, what would it look like?

4. When was a time that you tasted a personal victory? How did you feel?

5. When was a time that you tasted personal defeat? How did you feel?

TEAM EFFORT—JUNIOR HIGH/MIDDLE SCHOOL (15-20 MINUTES)

FAILURE IS NEVER FINAL: TWO PORTRAITS

• Give each student a copy of "Failure Is Never Final—Two Portraits" on pages 19-20 or display a copy using an overhead projector.

• Have a different student read each of the following portraits, then discuss the questions as a whole group.

• See reproducible for "Portraits."

1. What would have happened if Abraham Lincoln or Thomas Edison had let failure become final in their lives?

2. In your opinion, what was it that kept Abraham Lincoln and Thomas Edison from giving up after they had failed?

3. Why is it so easy to let failure get the best of us?

4. What are some ways you can turn defeats into victories?

TEAM EFFORT—HIGH SCHOOL (15-20 MINUTES)

PETER, THIS IS YOUR LIFE!

• Divide students into four smaller groups.

• Assign each group one of following scenes to role-play:

Scene One	John 1:35-42
Scene Two	Mark 14:27-31,66-72
Scene Three	Mark 16:6,7; John 21:15-19
Scene Four	Acts 2:14,22-24,36-41; 3:1-8

• Give the groups about 7 to 10 minutes to come up with a dramatic presentation of their scene from Peter's life. Encourage the groups to have fun, modernize and use their imaginations to present the story.

• Have each group perform their scene for the entire group. If possible, videotape the scenes and show them at a later time.

• Option: Use cheap trophies from a thrift store as awards for the "Best Interpretation" or "Best Modern Reenactment".

IN THE WORD (25-30 MINUTES)

PETER: FROM FAILURE TO FOLLOWER

• Divide students into groups of three or four.

• Give each student a copy of "Peter: From Failure to Follower" on pages 21-24 and a pen or pencil, or display a copy on an overhead projector.

• Have students complete the Bible study.

We're going to look at the life of one of the most well-known failures in the New Testament—Peter! Peter was one of Jesus' most outspoken followers. In fact, his mouth got him into quite a bit of trouble. Let's take a look at four scenes

from the life of Peter that prove in God's eyes that failure is never final!!!
Read each of the following passages and discuss the questions.

SCENE ONE: GOD SEES YOUR POTENTIAL (JOHN 1:40-42)
Read John 1:40-42.

1. Why do you think Jesus changed Simon's name to Peter?

2. What significance is there in Peter's name meaning "rock"?

3. How does it feel to know that God sees past your failures to your potential?

SCENE TWO: GOD KNOWS YOUR FAILURES (MARK 14:27-31,66-72)

1. How would you have felt if you were Peter...

Before denying Christ? (Mark 14:27-31)

After denying Christ? (Mark 14:66-72)

2. Has there ever been a time in your life when you felt either one of those ways?

3. Peter had promised to die for Jesus, yet when it came to putting his faith into action at the garden and in the courtyard, he faltered. Share about a time in your life when you have faltered like Peter.

4. God knows our weaknesses. Is that a comfort or a burden to you? Why?

SCENE THREE: GOD IS IN THE BUSINESS OF RESTORATION (MARK 16:6,7; JOHN 21:15-19)

1. What is the significance of the two words "and Peter" found in Mark 16:7?

2. How do you think Peter felt when he heard those two words?

3. Read John 21:15-19. If you were Peter, how would you have felt standing before Jesus...

As He asked you "Do you love me?"

As He restored you and said "Follow me"?

SCENE FOUR: GOD WANTS TO USE YOU (ACTS 2:36-41; 3:1-8)

1. How did God use Peter in Acts 2:36-41 and 3:1-8?

FAILURE IS NEVER FINAL—TWO PORTRAITS

The pages of history are filled with people who were once failures, but they are now legends. The difference in those who have led lives of excellence and those who have led lives of mediocrity lies in their willingness to fail and learn from their failures. Failure is not final; it's an opportunity to grow, learn and be used by God. Here's a look at two such people:

Portrait One:

1831   He failed in business.
1832   He was defeated in the legislature.
1833   He again failed in business.
1834   He was elected to the legislature.
1835   His wife-to-be died.
1836   He had a nervous breakdown.
1838   He was defeated for Speaker of the House.
1840   He was defeated for elector.
1850   A son died.
1855   He was defeated for the Senate.
1856   He was defeated for vice president.
1858   He was defeated for the Senate.
1860   This man, Abraham Lincoln, was elected president.[1]

Portrait Two:

In all the pages of history, there are few "failures" with the caliber of Thomas Edison. For years, Edison tried in vain to accomplish something that they said could never be done—create the light bulb! In actuality, Thomas Edison made over 900 attempts to create a light bulb before finding success. Over 900 times Edison developed a bulb, only to be sent back to the drawing board to try again. Over 900 times Edison was a failure, yet in the middle of all the failure, Edison tried and tried again. According to Thomas Edison, every time he experienced failure, he merely "found out one more way not to make a light bulb." Edison did not let failure become final for him; eventually he did create the light bulb and went down in the pages of history as one of the greatest inventors of all time!

1. What would have happened if Abraham Lincoln or Thomas Edison had let failure become final in their lives?

----

2. In your opinion, what was it that kept Abraham Lincoln and Thomas Edison from giving up after they had failed?

 © 1996 by Gospel Light. Permission to photocopy granted.

3. Why is it so easy to let failure get the best of us?

    ....

    ....

    ....

4. What are some ways you can turn defeats into victories?

    ....

    ....

    ....

1. Tim Hansel, *Holy Sweat* (Waco, Tex.: Word Publishing), p. 124.

 **IN THE WORD**

PETER: FROM FAILURE TO FOLLOWER

We're going to look at the life of one of the most well-known failures in the New Testament—Peter! Peter was one of Jesus' most outspoken followers. In fact, his mouth got him into quite a bit of trouble. Let's take a look at four scenes from the life of Peter that prove in God's eyes that failure is never final!!!

Read each of the following passages and discuss the questions.

Scene One: God Sees Your Potential (John 1:40-42)
Read John 1:40-42.

1. Why do you think Jesus changed Simon's name to Peter?

2. What significance is there in Peter's name meaning "rock"?

3. How does it feel to know that God sees past your failures to your potential?

Scene Two: God Knows Your Weaknesses and Failures (Mark 14:27-31,66-72)

1. How would you have felt if you were Peter...

   Before denying Christ? (Mark 14:27-31)

   After denying Christ? (Mark 14:66-72)

 © 1996 by Gospel Light. Permission to photocopy granted.

PETER:
FAILURE IS
NEVER FINAL

2. Has there ever been a time in your life when you felt either one of those ways?

....

....

....

3. Peter had promised to die for Jesus, yet when it came to putting his faith into action (at the garden and in the court-yard), he faltered. Share about a time in your life when you faltered like that.

....

....

....

4. God sees our weaknesses. Is that a comfort or a burden to you? Why?

....

....

Scene Three: God Is in the Business of Restoration (Mark 16:6,7; John 21:15-19)

1. What is the significance of the two words "and Peter" found in Mark 16:7?

....

....

....

2. How do you think Peter felt when he heard those two words?

....

....

....

3. Read John 21:15-19. If you were Peter, how would you have felt standing before Jesus...

    As He asked you, "Do you love me?"

....

....

    As He restored you and said "Follow me"?

....

....

....

© 1996 by Gospel Light. Permission to photocopy granted.

4. How does it affect you to know that God sees beyond your failures and can forgive and restore you?

....

....

Scene Four: God Wants to Use You (Acts 2:36-41; 3:1-8)

1. How did God use Peter in Acts 2:36-41 and 3:1-8?

....

....

What were the results of Peter's obedience?

....

....

2. Even though Peter felt like a failure, God used him as a part of His plan to touch lives. What hope can be found for you personally from these verses in Acts?

....

....

So What?

1. After looking at the four scenes, in what way can you relate to Peter?

....

....

2. What are some of your failures and weaknesses that you need to give over to God?

....

....

3. What are some of the areas of your life in which you desperately need to sense the restoration of God?

....

....

 © 1996 by Gospel Light. Permission to photocopy granted.

4. In what areas does God want to use you?

....

....

....

5. What are two things that you learned from this session?

....

....

....

What action step will you take to apply what you have learned about yourself?

....

....

....

© 1996 by Gospel Light. Permission to photocopy granted.

Things to Think About

1. Why is it so difficult to see past our weaknesses and failures to the potential God sees in us?

....
....
....

2. How does it feel to know that...

   God sees your potential?

....
....

   God knows your weaknesses and failures?

....
....

   God is in the business of restoration?

....
....

   God wants to use you?

....
....

3. How does 2 Corinthians 12:9,10 relate to your life and this session?

....
....
....

 © 1996 by Gospel Light. Permission to photocopy granted.

PETER:
FAILURE IS
NEVER FINAL

PARENT PAGE

IN THE CLASSROOM OF LIFE

Failure is the classroom of life. Even within the pages of God's Word failures can be seen as instruments God used to mold and change lives. Peter is perhaps the greatest failure found in the New Testament, yet God saw past his failures to the potential that was within him. God's ultimate desire was to use Peter in spite of his failures. His desire is the same for each of us.

Discuss the following statements as a family:

Failure is not an obstacle; it's just an opportunity.

"Success is never final. Failure is never fatal. It is courage that counts."
—Winston Churchill

"He who has never failed somewhere, that man cannot be great. Failure is the truest test of greatness."—F. D. Mattiesen

"There are a lot of ways to become a failure, but never taking a chance is the most successful."—Bob Phillips

Read the following Scriptures:
Mark 14:27-31,66-72
Mark 16:6,7; John 21:15-19
Acts 2:36-41

4. What are some areas right now in the life of your family that could be seen as failures?

....
....
....
....

5. How can you pray that God would use those failures as opportunities for growth and service to Him?

....
....
....
....

1. Why did God still choose to use Peter in spite of his denial of Christ?

....
....
....

2. Why is the story of Peter good news for imperfect people?

....
....
....
....

3. What are some areas of your life where failure has turned out to be an opportunity?

....
....
....
....

Session 1: "Peter: Failure Is Never Final"
Date ....

© 1996 by Gospel Light. Permission to photocopy granted.

PAUL:
HAVING A HEART FOR OTHERS

KEY VERSE

"We loved you so much that we were delighted to share with you not only the gospel of God but our lives as well, because you had become so dear to us." 1 Thessalonians 2:8

BIBLICAL BASIS

Matthew 18:20;
Luke 10:30-37;
Acts 4:36; 14:21,22;
1 Corinthians 13:4,8;
Galatians 2:1; 6:2;
Philippians 1:1-4;
1 Thessalonians 2:8,12;
1 Timothy 1:16;
Hebrews 10:24,25

THE BIG IDEA

The life of Paul was marked by his caring, sharing and encouragement of others. God is calling each of us to have that same servant's heart for others.

AIMS OF THIS SESSION

During this session, you will guide students to:
• Examine the life of Paul and his concern for others;
• Discover the hallmarks of a ministry of caring for others;
• Implement a lifestyle of caring, sharing and encouraging those around them.

WARM UP

WHO DO YOU LISTEN TO?—

A discussion and rating of those who have the most influence on students' lives.

TEAM EFFORT— JUNIOR HIGH/ MIDDLE SCHOOL

THE ADVENTURES OF MR. GOOD GUY AND MR. HAPPY TRAVELER—

Students perform a melodrama loosely based on the story of the Good Samaritan.

TEAM EFFORT— HIGH SCHOOL

LIVING IN THE REAL WORLD—

Students develop case studies for a discussion about real-life situations.

IN THE WORD

VITAL SIGNS: HAVING A HEARTBEAT FOR OTHERS—

A Bible study examining Paul's concern for the spiritual and personal needs of others.

THINGS TO THINK ABOUT (OPTIONAL)

Questions to get students thinking and talking about caring for, sharing with and encouraging others.

PARENT PAGE

A tool to get the session into the home and allow parents and young people to discuss how to develop a servant's heart for the needs of others.

PAUL:
HAVING A HEART
FOR OTHERS

LEADER'S DEVOTIONAL

"Fourteen years later I went up again to Jerusalem, this time with Barnabas. I took Titus along also" (Galatians 2:1).

Barnabas was a partner with Paul. Titus was a disciple of Paul's. Both men spent much time with Paul as they worked together to further the gospel of Christ. A striking aspect of Paul's ministry is not only his preaching of love to others "Love is patient, love is kind,…love never fails" (1 Corinthians 13:4,8), but also the proof of his love. Paul's commitment to Christ compelled him to be compassionate. Both his words and his ways revealed his heart for others. If you want to know a person's heart, don't just listen, watch.

Youth ministry, as modeled by the ministry of Paul, is a business of "going with" and "taking along also." Barnabas was the man whom Paul was "going with." Barnabas was a land baron who valued God's work more than his own worth (see Acts 4:36). He donated his money, his time and his heart to God's work in partnership with Paul. Who is your Barnabas? Who is your peer with whom you share your vision, your needs, your pain, your joys? My personal experience shows the finest relationships I have developed in nearly twenty years of ministry came from the people with whom I shared ministry. Paul had a heart for others and Barnabas was blessed by Paul's heart.

Youth ministry is a task of "taking along also." Titus was a younger disciple of Paul's, a man Paul refers to with these kindhearted words: "Titus, my true son, in our common faith" (Titus 1:4). Like a father to his son, Paul revealed his heart to Titus as they ministered together. Titus is later left behind by Paul in Crete to lead a ministry. There is no greater encouragement to a minister than to see your heart for Christ duplicated in your own disciples. Who is your Titus? With whom can you not only share the words of a teaching curriculum, but your very heart?

Next time you are going to minister somewhere, ask yourself, "Who can go with me as a partner?" or "Who can I also take with me as a disciple?" You may find a ministry more powerful, enjoyable and rewarding than you ever imagined. Remember: when two or three are gathered in His name, the King is in their midst (see Matthew 18:20). (Written by Doug Webster)

"The glory of friendship is not the outstretched hand, nor the kindly smile, nor the joy of companionship; it's the spiritual inspiration that comes to one when he discovers that someone else believes in him and is willing to trust him with his friendship."
—Ralph Waldo Emerson

PAUL:
HAVING A HEART FOR OTHERS

KEY VERSE

"We loved you so much that we were delighted to share with you not only the gospel of God but our lives as well, because you had become so dear to us." 1 Thessalonians 2:8

BIBLICAL BASIS

Matthew 18:20; Luke 10:30-37; Acts 4:36; 14:21,22; 1 Corinthians 13:4,8; Galatians 2:1; 6:2; Philippians 1:1-4; 1 Thessalonians 2:8,12; 1 Timothy 1:16; Hebrews 10:24,25

THE BIG IDEA

The life of Paul was marked by his caring, sharing and encouragement of others. God is calling each of us to have that same servant's heart for others.

WARM UP (5-10 MINUTES)

Who Do You Listen To?

• Divide the students into groups of three or four.
• Give each student a copy of "Who Do You Listen To?" on page 31 and a pen or pencil.
• Have students share their answers with the other members of their small groups.
Rate the following people in your life according to their influence and impact on you on a scale from 1 to 6 (1 = the most influence or impact and 6 = the least influence or impact on you).

   ___ Teachers   ___ Friend
   ___ Pastor   ___ Parents
   ___ Youth Leader   ___ Other:

1. Who has influenced you the most or has impacted your life the most?

2. What have they done to impact your life?

3. Why have they had such a big impact on your life?

4. Who has had the least influence or impact? Why?

---- Fold ----

Part of encouragement is seeing others as God sees them. God sees incredible potential in everyone. The job of encouragers is to help those around them see what God sees in them and live out that potential in their lives.

1. Who has encouraged you lately and in what way have you been encouraged?

2. How does encouragement affect...

Someone's view of him- or herself?

His or her view of God?

His or her spiritual growth?

3. What keeps us from encouraging others more often?

4. What are some practical ways that you can encourage others in their relationships with God?

SO WHAT?
1. Who in your life needs to feel cared for? What can you do about it?

Person:

Action:

2. What has God been doing in your life?

Who needs to hear about it?

3. Who in your life needs to hear about the gospel of God? What action can you take?

Person:

Action:

THINGS TO THINK ABOUT (OPTIONAL)

• Use the questions on page 39 after or as a part of "In the Word."
1. Why is it difficult to care for some people?
2. How would you define the word "encouragement"?
3. How does encouragement help people see what God sees in them?
4. Which of the three areas—caring, sharing or encouragement—do you need to work on the most?

PARENT PAGE

• Distribute page to parents.

THE ADVENTURES OF MR. GOOD GUY AND MR. HAPPY TRAVELER

- Prepare the props beforehand and have them available.
- Select 10 people to be a part of this melodrama. Be sure to select people who feel comfortable doing some pretty outrageous things in front of the group.
- After you have selected the students and assigned the characters, have them stand "offstage" until they are "read" into the scene. Be sure to remind them that the more creative and outgoing they are, the better the melodrama will be. The key to a good melodrama is pausing and emphasizing when you read it to the group. You may also want to personalize it a little, by adding or adapting jokes to your group (include any "inside jokes" your group may have).

A melodrama loosely based on Luke 10:30-37.

CHARACTERS:

1 Mr. Happy Traveler	1 church leader from the first Church of Jericho
1 tree	1 Mr. Good Guy
3 thugs	1 Buck, the donkey
1 pastor	1 Harry, the innkeeper

PROPS:

1 "Jerusalem—5 miles or so" sign	1 glass of water
1 "Jericho—down 3 miles to the left" sign	1 "Harry's Roadside Hotel—1 mile" sign and someone in the
2 tree branches for the person who plays the tree	audience to throw it on stage
1 "Tree" sign for the tree	1 welcome mat

(On stage is the lone tree, holding two branches and a sign that says "tree", and two signs, one pointing toward Jerusalem and the other pointing toward Jericho.)

After the melodrama, have your group turn to Luke 10:30-37 for the real story of what happened. Let them know that during your time together, you're going to explore what it means to have a heart for others by looking at the life of Paul.

LIVING IN THE REAL WORLD

- Divide students into groups of three or four.
- Give each group a sheet of paper and a pen or pencil. Assign one person in each group as the group's secretary.
- Tell the groups that they have about five minutes to come up with a "real-life" situation or case study dealing with some problem, issue or crisis. Have them end the case study with "What would you do?" Each group's secretary should write down a brief description of the situation.
- Have the groups exchange case studies and give them 10 minutes to read and respond to the case study. Encourage them to add any Scriptures that might help in dealing with the person, situation or problem. After the allotted time, have the group members share their answers to the following questions:

1. **What was the case study you were given?**
   What would you do if you were in that situation?

2. **What are some Scriptures that would help you in dealing with that situation?**

3. What are some characteristics of someone who has a heart for others?
4. What are some roadblocks that keep you from caring more for the needs of others?

VITAL SIGNS: HAVING A HEARTBEAT FOR OTHERS

- Divide students into groups of three or four.
- Give each student a copy of "Vital Signs: Having a Heartbeat for Others" on pages 35-38 and a pen or pencil, or display a copy on an overhead projector.
- Have students complete the Bible study.

Paul's life was marked by an incredible heart for helping and encouraging others. From Jerusalem, to Syria, to Asia, to Macedonia and all the way to Rome, Paul took care of the needs of others. His passion was to see people changed by the incredible love of God. God is calling us to that same mission of caring for, sharing with and encouraging others.

CARING FOR OTHERS

"We loved you so much that we were delighted to share with you not only the gospel of God but our lives as well, because you had become so dear to us" (1 Thessalonians 2:8).

1. What motivated Paul to share his life with others?
   ....

2. What are some characteristics of someone with a caring heart?
   ....

3. How have you felt God's care for you?
   ....

4. What are some practical ways to care for those around us?
   ....

SHARING WITH OTHERS

"But for that very reason I was shown mercy so that in me, the worst of sinners, Christ Jesus might display his unlimited patience as an example for those who believe on him and receive eternal life" (1 Timothy 1:16).

1. What are two things that Paul shared with others?
   ....

2. Why is it difficult to share our lives with others?
   ....
   Why is it difficult to share the gospel with others?
   ....

3. How does sharing the gospel and sharing our lives go hand-in-hand?
   ....

4. What are some practical ways you can share what God has been doing in your life?
   ....

5. What are some practical ways to share the Good News of Jesus Christ?
   ....

ENCOURAGING OTHERS

"Encouraging, comforting and urging you to live lives worthy of God, who calls you into his kingdom and glory" (1 Thessalonians 2:12).

"Then they returned to Lystra, Iconium and Antioch, strengthening the disciples and encouraging them to remain true to the faith" (Acts 14:21,22).

 WARM UP

WHO DO YOU LISTEN TO?

Rate the following people in your life according to their influence and impact on you on a scale from 1 to 6 (1 = the most influence or impact, and 6 = the least influence or impact on you).

_____ Teachers

_____ Pastor

_____ Youth Leader

_____ Friend _____

_____ Parents

_____ Other: _____

1. Who has influenced you the most or has impacted your life the most?

....

....

....

2. What have they done to impact your life?

....

....

....

3. Why have they had such a big impact on your life?

....

....

....

4. Who has had the least influence or impact? Why?

....

....

....

 © 1996 by Gospel Light. Permission to photocopy granted.

TEAM EFFORT

THE ADVENTURES OF MR. GOOD GUY AND MR. HAPPY TRAVELER

A melodrama loosely based on Luke 10:30-37.

Characters:

1 Mr. Happy Traveler
1 tree
3 thugs
1 pastor
1 church leader from the First Church of Jericho
1 Mr. Good Guy
1 Buck, the donkey
1 Harry, the innkeeper

Props:

1 "Jerusalem—5 miles or so" sign
1 "Jericho—down 3 miles to the left" sign
2 tree branches for the person who plays the tree
1 "Tree" sign for the tree
1 glass of water
1 "Harry's Roadside Hotel—1 mile" sign and someone in audience to throw it on stage
1 welcome mat
(On stage is the lone tree, holding two branches and a sign that says "tree", and two signs, one pointing toward Jerusalem and the other pointing toward Jericho)

One very fine day, a man was traveling along the roadside, minding his own business, singing a happy tune. He was a very fine singer. The audience applauded. Mr. Happy Traveler took a bow.

Since it was early in the morning, Mr. Happy Traveler was stretching and doing deep knee bends while he continued to sing.

All of a sudden, peering from behind the tree were three of the meanest, toughest, most ruthless thugs in all the land. As they sneered and flexed from behind the tree, each one looking more mean and nasty than the other, the thugs had a disagreement and began to fight amongst themselves.

Mr. Happy Traveler heard the noise. He stopped his singing and deep knee bends and said, "Harketh, who goeth thereth?" Just then the thugs froze with peculiar smiles on their faces. Mr. Happy Traveler began singing a happy tune again.

Quietly, the thugs crept up on Mr. Happy Traveler and jumped him, beating him senseless (well, almost senseless). After the thugs had done their deed, they stood up, leaving Mr. Happy Traveler in a heap on the floor, just smiling now instead of singing. They looked around in amazement as the voice of the narrator said, "Now that you've beaten Mr. Happy Traveler, what are you going to do next?"

© 1996 by Gospel Light. Permission to photocopy granted.

"We're gonna go to Disneyland!" they proclaimed as they exited, leaping and skipping from the stage.

As Mr. Happy Traveler lay groaning on the floor (let Mr. Happy Traveler groan for a while), along came the pastor from the local church whistling a praise song. The pastor was so oblivious to Mr. Happy Traveler that he tripped over him. The pastor apologized. Mr. Happy Traveler groaned, "That's okay."

The pastor knelt down near Mr. Happy Traveler to see if he was still alive. He checked his pulse. The pastor jumped to his feet and proclaimed, "He's alive! He's alive! He's alive!!!" Bending over, the pastor asked Mr. Happy Traveler, "Pardon me, do you know how I can get to the First Church of Jerusalem? I'm late, I'm late for a very important date!" The audience groaned because it was a dumb joke. Mr. Happy Traveler groaned and pointed to the sign. The pastor thanked him and left for Jerusalem, whistling another praise song.

As Mr. Happy Traveler lay groaning again only this time louder (let Mr. Happy Traveler groan for a longer time), along came a leader of the First Church of Jericho, hurrying along and mumbling to himself. Without knowing it, the church leader tripped over Mr. Happy Traveler. Scrambling to his feet, the church leader apologized. Mr. Happy Traveler groaned, "That's okay."

The church leader, noticing that Mr. Happy Traveler needed some help, began to quote verses from the Bible to comfort Mr. Happy Traveler (let the church leader go for a little while). After exhausting all the verses he knew and looking around for some help, the church leader began to sing "Kum-ba-ya." The audience joined in. The church leader, feeling proud for a job well done, patted himself on the back. The audience stopped singing the annoying song. The church leader bent over Mr. Happy Traveler and said, "Yea verily, verily I beseech thee. (pause) Couldst thou tell me where I might find the Jerusalem 7-11? With all this singing, I'm dying for a Big Gulp!" The audience in unison pointed toward Jerusalem. The church leader thanked the audience and exited toward Jerusalem saying, "Oh, thank heaven for 7-11!!!"

As Mr. Happy Traveler lay groaning for a third time, this time even louder, along came Mr. Good Guy and his sidekick, Buck the donkey. The audience applauded loudly. Now Mr. Good Guy was watching where he was walking and did not trip over Mr. Happy Traveler. Mr. Happy Traveler thanked Mr. Good Guy. "You're welcome," replied Mr. Good Guy.

Mr. Good Guy bent down over Mr. Happy Traveler. He had pity and compassion on him, saying, "Poor Mr. Happy Traveler." The audience mimicked, "Poor Mr. Happy Traveler." He took Traveler's pulse and poured water on him. Then picking up Mr. Happy Traveler with a grunt, Mr. Good Guy placed Mr. Happy Traveler ever so gently on his trusted donkey, Buck. Buck groaned (pause) and said, "I hate this job." Buck and Mr. Good Guy then ventured high and low in search of the local inn. "I know what we need," cried Mr. Good Guy. "A sign." ("Harry's Roadside Hotel—1 mile" sign is thrown from the audience onto the stage.) The audience groaned because it was yet another dumb joke.

Going further, they met Harry the Innkeeper, who was holding out the welcome mat (Harry holds the welcome mat). Harry said, "Hello, Mr. Good Guy. Hello, Buck. Who's the guy with the smile on his face?"

© 1996 by Gospel Light. Permission to photocopy granted.

"This is Mr. Happy Traveler," said Mr. Good Guy, waving Mr. Happy Traveler's hand. "Could you look after him for me and if he needs anything, put it on my American Express Card; I never leave home without it." Mr. Good Guy placed Mr. Happy Traveler ever so gently on the doorstep of Harry's Roadside Hotel and with his best Arnold Schwarzeneggar impersonation said, "I'll be back!"

As Mr. Good Guy and Buck turned to take off into the sunset, Harry the Innkeeper exclaimed, "What a good guy!" The audience joined in, "What a good guy!" And all the people said, "The end!"

© 1996 by Gospel Light. Permission to photocopy granted.

**PAUL:
HAVING A HEART
FOR OTHERS**

VITAL SIGNS: HAVING A HEARTBEAT FOR OTHERS

Paul's life was marked by an incredible heart for helping and encouraging others. From Jerusalem, to Syria, to Asia, to Macedonia and all the way to Rome, Paul took care of the needs of others. His passion was to see people changed by the incredible love of God. God is calling us to that same mission of caring for, sharing with and encouraging others.

Caring for Others

"We loved you so much that we were delighted to share with you not only the gospel of God but our lives as well, because you had become so dear to us." (1 Thessalonians 2:8).

1. What motivated Paul to share his life with others?

2. What are some characteristics of someone with a caring heart?

3. How have you felt God's care for you?

4. What are some practical ways to care for those around us?

Sharing with Others

"But for that very reason I was shown mercy so that in me, the worst of sinners, Christ Jesus might display his unlimited patience as an example for those who believe on him and receive eternal life" (1 Timothy 1:16).

1. What are two things that Paul shared with others?

 © 1996 by Gospel Light. Permission to photocopy granted.

2. Why is it difficult to share the gospel of God with others?

....

....

....

Why is it difficult to share our lives with others?

....

....

....

3. How does sharing the gospel and sharing our lives go hand-in-hand?

....

....

....

4. What are some practical ways you can share what God has been doing in your life?

....

....

....

5. What are some practical ways to share the Good News of Jesus Christ?

....

....

....

Encouraging Others

"Encouraging, comforting and urging you to live lives worthy of God, who calls you into his kingdom and glory" (1 Thessalonians 2:12).

"Then they returned to Lystra, Iconium and Antioch, strengthening the disciples and encouraging them to remain true to the faith" (Acts 14:21-22).

Part of encouragement is seeing others as God sees them. God sees incredible potential in everyone. The job of encouragers is to help those around them see what God sees in them and live out that potential in their lives.

1. Who has encouraged you lately and in what way have you been encouraged?

....

....

....

2. How does encouragement affect...

Someone's view of him- or herself?

....

....

His or her view of God?

....

....

His or her spiritual growth?

....

....

3. What keeps us from encouraging others more often?

....

....

4. What are some practical ways that you can encourage others in their relationships with God?

....

....

So What?

1. Who in your life needs to feel cared for? What can you do about it?

Person: ....

Action: ....

....

....

 © 1996 by Gospel Light. Permission to photocopy granted.

**PAUL:
HAVING A HEART
FOR OTHERS**

2. What has God been doing in your life?

....

....

....

Who needs to hear about it?

....

....

....

3. Who in your life needs to hear about the gospel of God? What action will you take?

Person: ....

Action:

....

....

....

© 1996 by Gospel Light. Permission to photocopy granted.

*T*HINGS TO THINK ABOUT

1. Why is it difficult to care for some people?

....

....

....

2. How would you define the word "encouragement"?

....

....

....

3. How does encouragement help people see what God sees in them?

....

....

....

4. Which of the three areas—caring, sharing or encouragement—do you need to work on the most?

....

....

....

 © 1996 by Gospel Light. Permission to photocopy granted.

**PAUL:
HAVING A HEART
FOR OTHERS**

PARENT PAGE

STATE OF THE HEART

The life of Paul is one that is marked by a deep concern for others. God is calling us to "look not only to [our] own interests, but also to the interests of others" (Philippians 2:4). In a real sense, we are the hands, feet and voice of Jesus in this world. When we reach out to others with a heart of deep concern, lives are changed.

Complete the following statements.

1. The most others-centered person I know is .... , because...

2. The time that I felt the most encouraged by someone was when...

3. The time I felt that God used me in another person's life the most was when...

4. One time when I got to share my life and faith with someone was...

5. When I reach out and help others, I feel...

6. One person I know who needs to be encouraged is .... , because...

© 1996 by Gospel Light. Permission to photocopy granted.

**PAUL:
HAVING A HEART
FOR OTHERS**

7. One person I know who needs to be shared with is .... , because...

....

....

....

8. Check out the following verses. What do they say about having a heart for others?

....

....

....

Galatians 6:2

....

....

....

Philippians 2:1-4

....

....

....

1 Thessalonians 2:8,12

....

....

....

Hebrews 10:24,25

....

....

....

9. What will you do this week to have more of a servant's heart for those outside your family?

....

....

....

10. What will you do this week to be more of a servant to those inside your family?

....

....

Session 2: "Paul: Having a Heart for
Others" Date ....

 © 1996 by Gospel Light. Permission to photocopy granted.

TIMOTHY:
A WORTHY EXAMPLE

Key Verse

"Don't let anyone look down on you because you are young, but set an example for the believers in speech, in life, in love, in faith and in purity." 1 Timothy 4:12

Biblical Basis

1 Corinthians 6:18-20;
Ephesians 4:1,29;
1 Thessalonians 2:11,12;
1 Timothy 4:12;
2 Timothy 2:2,22; 4:7;
1 John 3:16-18; 4:7-12

The Big Idea

God is looking for young people who will be bold examples of what it means to live out their faith in Christ in today's world.

Aims of This Session

During this session, you will guide students to:
• Examine how Paul challenged Timothy and every Christian to be examples for others;
• Discover how their examples impact those around them for Christ;
• Implement a decision to live their lives as examples of integrity to others.

Warm Up

If I...—
Students complete statements about improbable situations.

Team Effort— Junior High/ Middle School

What Would You Do?—
Students discuss what their response as Christians should be to a variety of real-life situations.

Team Effort— High School

What Do You Think?—
A discussion about whether or not actions do speak louder than words.

In the Word

Your Life Is Speaking So Loud I Can't Hear a Word You're Saying!—
A Bible study on Paul's challenge to Timothy to live his life as an example for others.

Things to Think About (Optional)

Questions to get students thinking and talking about the fact that setting a good example has no age limits.

Parent Page

A tool to get the session into the home and allow parents and young people to discuss their family's level of integrity.

TIMOTHY:
A WORTHY
EXAMPLE

LEADER'S DEVOTIONAL

**"Entrust to reliable men who will also be qualified to teach others"
(2 Timothy 2:2).**

"Sure, I'll do that in the morning."

Those words came ringing back into my head just now as I hear the water running. You see, my wife asked me last night if I would reprogram the sprinkler system to run three times a day instead of once. We reseeded the lawn to cover the spots left by our new dog Molly. The dog is doing just fine, but the grass is burned every time she shows up.

More often in my wife's experience than I'd like to admit, her concern has less to do with the dog showing up and more to do with Doug not showing up. When I promise and I don't deliver, I leave a burn mark on my integrity. Granted in this case, my wife will likely offer me forgiveness as I shuffle downstairs with my tail between my legs, groveling at her feet and begging for mercy. She'll reach into "Doug's emotional bowl" and pull out stored up reliability to cover for my "oops." If I continue to promise and not deliver, my family is left with the perpetual task of covering Dad's spots.

There's something far worse than a family member or friend covering for us when we don't come through. It's called shattered hope. When we receive a promise, we place hope in the form of an expectation. When the promise fizzles, the expectation is dashed. An emotional withdrawal is taken from the heart. Unless you have an abundance of emotional deposits in the heart of the recipient, you'll find yourself overdrawn. Beyond the relational deficit, something else happens—we lose our integrity. The absence of integrity causes feelings of hopelessness.

The power of the promise kept is the crux of the gospel. God said He would deliver and He gave us His Son. Jesus told us ahead of time and He came through the Resurrection as He promised. Paul knew when he entrusted his commands to Timothy, young Tim would deliver. He was a man of integrity. Paul advised Timothy, "Entrust to reliable men who will also be qualified to teach others" (2 Timothy 2:2).

People with integrity gain the trust from the leader that they will carry through on the task. People with integrity offer promises. People who promise offer hope. People who deliver on a promise fulfill hope and build integrity. People with integrity, like Timothy, gain the trust and get the commission from God.

Now, excuse me. I have a sprinkler system to program, a lawn to water and some integrity to restore. With a few vital steps, I can avoid changing the doghouse to the "Doughouse."
(Written by Doug Webster)

**"The reputation of a thousand years may be determined by the conduct of one hour."
—Japanese proverb**

TIMOTHY: A WORTHY EXAMPLE

✓ KEY VERSE

"Don't let anyone look down on you because you are young, but set an example for the believers in speech, in life, in love, in faith and in purity." 1 Timothy 4:12

B IBLICAL BASIS

1 Corinthians 6:18-20; Ephesians 4:1,29; 1 Thessalonians 2:11,12; 1 Timothy 4:12; 2 Timothy 2:2,22; 4:7; 1 John 3:16-18; 4:7-12

✓ THE BIG IDEA

God is looking for young people who will be bold examples of what it means to live out their faith in Christ in today's world.

W ARM UP (5-10 MINUTES)

If I...

• Give each student a copy of "If I..." on pages 47-48 and a pen or pencil.
• Have students complete as many of the statements as possible in three minutes.
• Have students share their completions of at least one of the statements.

Complete the following statements:

1. If I won the lottery, I'd...
2. If I could travel anywhere, I'd go to...
3. If I could be anyone in the world, I'd be...
4. If I could be any cartoon character, I'd be...
5. If I could be any animal, I'd be...
6. If I could have any job in the world, I'd...
7. If I had a month to live, I'd...
8. If I could spend an hour face-to-face with God, I'd...
9. If I had the power to go back in time, I'd...
10. If I _____ I'd...

---- Fold ----

2. Why can faith sometimes be a fight?

3. What are some of the fights you have in keeping your faith?

4. What are some practical ways to keep the faith and strengthen it?

PURITY

Read 1 Corinthians 6:18-20.

1. What are some of the influences that challenge the purity of today's teenager?

2. How should knowing that your body is the temple of the Holy Spirit affect your thoughts about staying pure?

3. How can we honor God with our bodies?

SO WHAT?

1. Rate your life on a scale of 1 to 10 on being an example in the following areas (1 = needs lots of work and 10 = doing great):

Speech									
1	2	3	4	5	6	7	8	9	10
Life									
1	2	3	4	5	6	7	8	9	10
Love									
1	2	3	4	5	6	7	8	9	10
Faith									
1	2	3	4	5	6	7	8	9	10
Purity									
1	2	3	4	5	6	7	8	9	10

✓ 2. Which one of the five areas do you need to work on the most in your life?

3. What will you do about it? What are two action steps you can take to work on that area?

Action Step One:

Action Step Two:

T HINGS TO THINK ABOUT (OPTIONAL)

• Use the questions on page 55 after or as a part of "In the Word."

1. Why do you think some people look down on the young

2. If Paul were here today, how would he rewrite 1 Timothy 4:12 to challenge Christian teenagers today?

3. What are some areas in which students today most need integrity?

P ARENT PAGE

• Distribute page to parents.

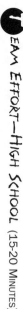

TEAM EFFORT—JUNIOR HIGH/MIDDLE SCHOOL (15-20 MINUTES)

WHAT WOULD YOU DO?

- Divide students into groups of three or four.
- Give each group a copy of "What Would You Do?" on pages 49-50.
- Have the groups discuss each situation.
- Discuss the questions at the bottom of the page with the whole group.
- Option: Divide students into five groups and give each group one of the situations from which to prepare two skits—one to show what most people would do and one to show what a Christian should do.

How should you as a Christian respond in the following situations?

1. **You see a group of your friends at lunch and decide to sit down and eat with them.** During the conversation, it turns from stuff about school and friends into a slam session on one of your friends who isn't there. As people continue ripping on the person, they look at you and ask "What do you think?"

2. **You are at a party with some of your friends and as the night progresses, you notice that there's more and more drinking going on.** You decide that you'll try to avoid it, so you move to a group that is standing by the sliding glass door. After a few minutes of talking with the group, someone walks up to you and hands you a beer. The group you are with looks at you to see your response.

3. **You and some of your friends are at a friend's house spending the night.** It's late and you're checking out what's on television. As someone starts flipping the channels on the cable, an "Adults Only" channel comes on. Your friend sets down the remote control. As the group settles in to watch the latest feature, you begin to feel awkward and the rest of the group can sense it.

4. **It's third period and you're in your math class, and you are taking a major test that you studied really hard for.** As you get the test, you look it over and your mind has gone blank. In a panic, you look at the girl next to you who is busily working on the test. As you look down, you can see her test. You begin to quickly scan the page that she is working on to try to pick up some of the answers to the questions you're struggling with when you sense something wrong.

5. **It's lunchtime and after picking up your lunch, you begin to leave with your friends to find the rest of the group.** As you make it to the far end of the lunch area, you see the boy who sits behind you in history class sitting by himself and looking a little lonely. As you pause by his table, your friends call out to you that they've found the rest of the group.

TEAM EFFORT—HIGH SCHOOL (15-20 MINUTES)

WHAT DO YOU THINK?

- Construct signs out of poster board or banner paper that say the following: "Agree," "Disagree" and "Strongly Disagree," "Strongly Agree,"
- Place the signs on the four walls of your meeting area.
- As you read the following statements, have the students stand under (or near) the sign that represents their opinion.
- After the students have selected their opinions, have some of those expressing the different opinions discuss why they feel that way.

1. You only believe as much as you live.
2. The world has the right to judge whether or not there is a God by the way we live our lives.

Read 1 Timothy 4:12.
1. Why is it tough to live out what you believe?
2. What kind of example do you need to set for others? Why?
3. Why do your actions impact others more than what you say?

Fold

46

---

3. Your words have more impact than your actions.
4. The problem with Christians today is we don't live what we talk.
5. How you live impacts how others see God.

IN THE WORD (25-30 MINUTES)

YOUR LIFE IS SPEAKING SO LOUD I CAN'T HEAR A WORD YOU'RE SAYING!

- Divide students into groups of three or four.
- Give each student a copy of "Your Life Is Speaking So Loud I Can't Hear a Word You're Saying" on pages 51-54 and a pen or pencil, or display a copy on an overhead projector.
- Have students complete the Bible study.

How we live our lives influences how those around us see God. Through the example of how we live, the gospel can become attractive to others. Paul challenges Timothy to live his life as an example for others. He challenges Timothy in five areas of life.

Read 1 Timothy 4:12.

SPEECH
Read Ephesians 4:29.
1. How do our words affect our example?

2. How do our words affect those around us?

3. Complete the following list with some examples of destructive words and constructive words:

Destructive Words	Constructive Words

LIFE
Read Ephesians 4:1 and 1 Thessalonians 2:11,12.
1. What does a "life worthy of the calling" mean to you?

2. In what ways should our lifestyles be different because we are followers of Jesus Christ?

LOVE
Read 1 John 4:7-12.
1. What are some of the words that describe God's love for us?

2. What keeps us from loving others with that same type of love?

3. How would a lifestyle of love impact those around us?

4. How does 1 John 3:16-18 challenge us to show love?

FAITH
Read 2 Timothy 4:7.
1. What did Paul mean in verse 7?

WARM UP

IF I...
Complete the following statements:

1. If I won the lottery, I'd...

2. If I could travel anywhere, I'd go...

3. If I could be anyone in the world, I'd be...

4. If I could be any cartoon character, I'd be...

5. If I could be any animal, I'd be...

6. If I could have any job in the world, I'd...

7. If I had a month to live, I'd...

 © 1996 by Gospel Light. Permission to photocopy granted.

8. If I could spend an hour face-to-face with God, I'd...

....

....

....

9. If I had the power to go back in time, I'd...

....

....

....

10. If I _____ , I'd...

....

....

....

*T*EAM *E*FFORT

WHAT WOULD YOU DO?

1. You see a group of your friends at lunch and decide to sit down and eat with them. During the conversation, it turns from stuff about school and friends into a slam session on one of your friends who isn't there. As people continue ripping on the person, they look at you and ask "What do you think?"

2. You are at a party with some of your friends and as the night progresses, you notice that there's more and more drinking going on. You decide that you'll try to avoid it, so you move to a group that is standing by the sliding glass door. After a few minutes of talking with the group, someone walks up to you and hands you a beer. The group you are with looks at you to see your response.

3. You and some of your friends are at a friend's house spending the night. It's late and you're checking out what's on television. As someone starts flipping the channels on the cable, an "Adults Only" channel comes on. Your friend sets down the remote control. As the group settles in to watch the latest feature, you begin to feel awkward and the rest of the group can sense it.

4. It's third period and you're in your math class, and you are taking a major test that you studied really hard for. As you get the test, you look it over and your mind goes blank. In a panic, you look at the girl next to you, who is busily working on the test. As you look down, you can see her test. You begin to quickly scan the page that she is working on to pick up some of the answers to the questions you're struggling with when you sense something wrong.

5. It's lunchtime and after picking up your lunch, you begin to leave with a friend to find the rest of the group. As you make it to the far end of the lunch area, you see the boy who sits behind you in history class sitting by himself and looking a little lonely. As you pause by his table, your friends call out to you that they've found the rest of the group.

 © 1996 by Gospel Light. Permission to photocopy granted.

TIMOTHY:
A WORTHY
EXAMPLE

Read 1 Timothy 4:12.

1. Why is it tough to live out what we believe?

....
....
....

2. What kind of example do we need to set for others? Why?

....
....
....

3. Why do your actions impact others more than what you say?

....
....
....

IN THE WORD

YOUR LIFE IS SPEAKING SO LOUD I CAN'T HEAR A WORD YOU'RE SAYING!

How we live our lives influences how those around us see God. Through the example of how we live, the gospel can become attractive to others. Paul challenges Timothy to live his life as an example for others. He challenges Timothy in five areas of life.
Read 1 Timothy 4:12.

Speech

Read Ephesians 4:29.

1. How do our words affect our example?

2. How do our words affect those around us?

3. Complete the following list with some examples of destructive words and constructive words:

Destructive Words	Constructive Words

Life

Read Ephesians 4:1 and 1 Thessalonians 2:11,12.

1. What does a "life worthy of the calling" mean to you?

 © 1996 by Gospel Light. Permission to photocopy granted.

2. In what ways should our lifestyles be different because we are followers of Jesus Christ?

....

....

Love

Read 1 John 4:7-12.

1. What are some of the words that describe God's love for us?

....

....

2. What keeps us from loving others with that same type of love?

....

....

3. How would a lifestyle of love impact those around us?

....

....

4. How does 1 John 3:16-18 challenge us to show love?

....

....

Faith

Read 2 Timothy 4:7.

1. What did Paul mean in verse 7?

....

....

2. Why can faith sometimes be a fight?

....

....

3. What are some of the fights you have in keeping your faith?

....

....

4. What are some practical ways to keep the faith and strengthen it?

....

....

Purity
Read 1 Corinthians 6:18-20.

1. What are some of the influences that challenge the purity of today's teenager?

....

....

2. How should knowing that your body is the temple of the Holy Spirit affect your thoughts on staying pure?

....

....

3. How can we honor God with our bodies?

....

....

 © 1996 by Gospel Light. Permission to photocopy granted.

**TIMOTHY:
A WORTHY
EXAMPLE**

So What?

1. Rate your life on a scale of 1 to 10 on being an example in the following areas (1 = needs lots of work and 10 = doing great):

Speech

| 1 | 2 | 3 | 4 | 5 | 6 | 7 | 8 | 9 | 10 |

Life

| 1 | 2 | 3 | 4 | 5 | 6 | 7 | 8 | 9 | 10 |

Love

| 1 | 2 | 3 | 4 | 5 | 6 | 7 | 8 | 9 | 10 |

Faith

| 1 | 2 | 3 | 4 | 5 | 6 | 7 | 8 | 9 | 10 |

Purity

| 1 | 2 | 3 | 4 | 5 | 6 | 7 | 8 | 9 | 10 |

2. Which one of the five areas do you need to work on the most in your life?

....

....

....

3. What will you do about it? What are two action steps you can take to work on that area?

....

....

Action Step One: ....

Action Step Two: ....

© 1996 by Gospel Light. Permission to photocopy granted.

THINGS TO THINK ABOUT

1. Why do you think some people look down on the young?

....
....
....

2. If Paul were here today, how would he rewrite 1 Timothy 4:12 to challenge Christian teenagers today?

....
....
....

3. What are some areas in which students today most need integrity?

....
....
....

 © 1996 by Gospel Light. Permission to photocopy granted.

TIMOTHY:
A WORTHY
EXAMPLE

PARENT PAGE

INTEGRITY INVENTORY

"Don't let anyone look down on you because you are young, but set an example for the believers in speech, in life, in love, in faith and in purity" (1 Timothy 4:12).

One of the greatest ways to impact the world and those around you is by living a godly life. When others see your faith lived out in your everyday life, it brings credibility and an attractiveness to the gospel. Take a few minutes and do an integrity inventory of your family on a scale of 1 to 10 (1 = needs some help in this area and 10 = this area going well). Complete the inventory and the questions individually, then discuss them as a family.

Speech
Read Ephesians 4:29.

_____ My words are marked by honesty.

_____ The words I say build others up instead of tearing them down.

_____ When I make a promise, I keep it.

1. Using the scale below, how would you rate your speech to one another in your family and to others?

Destructive   Constructive

1   2   3   4   5   6   7   8   9   10

2. How can you, as a family, be an example in the words that you speak to one another?

....

....

Life

_____ What I believe impacts how I live my life.

_____ I seek to live a life of integrity.

_____ I regularly consider how my life reflects what I believe and what I say.

1. Using the scale below, how would you rate the way you live your life around your family and others?

Destructive   Constructive

1   2   3   4   5   6   7   8   9   10

2. What are some areas you need to examine in your family life as an issue of integrity?

....

....

....

Love
Read 1 John 3:16-18.

_____ I seek to see others through the eyes of Jesus Christ.

_____ I seek to love others with my actions and not just my words.

_____ I am currently involved in some action that is expressing my love for others.

TIMOTHY:
A WORTHY
EXAMPLE

1. Using the scale below, how would you rate the way you show love to others in your family and those outside your family?

Very weak   Very strong

1   2   3   4   5   6   7   8   9   10

2. What can you be involved in as individuals or as a family to be more actively involved in loving others?

....

....

....

Faith

Read 2 Timothy 4:7.

_____   I sense a deepening of my faith and love relationship with Christ.

_____   I am involved in activities that help deepen my faith and love relationship with Christ.

1. Using the scale below, how would you rate the depth of your faith in the presence of your family and others?

Shallow   Deep

1   2   3   4   5   6   7   8   9   10

2. How can that affect those around you?

....

....

Purity

Read 1 Corinthians 6:18-20.

_____   I seem to have a pure heart before God.

_____   The things that I put into my mind, heart and soul encourage purity.

_____   I desire to "honor God with my body".

1. Using the scale below, how would you rate your level of purity in the presence of your family and others?

Impure   Pure

1   2   3   4   5   6   7   8   9   10

2. What can you do to promote purity in your family?

....

....

....

Session 3: "Timothy: A Worthy Example"

Date _____

 © 1996 by Gospel Light. Permission to photocopy granted.

MARY:
ORDINARY PERSON, EXTRAORDINARY FAITH

KEY VERSE

"'Blessed is she who has believed that what the Lord has said to her will be accomplished!'" Luke 1:45

BIBLICAL BASIS

Matthew 1:18-25; 17:20,21;
Luke 1:26-38; 45-56; 2:34,35;
John 2:1,3,5;
Romans 4:20,21;
Philippians 4:13;
2 Timothy 1:12;
Hebrews 11:1;
James 2:17

THE BIG IDEA

God is looking for people of faith—ordinary people who will place themselves in the hands of an extraordinary God.

AIMS OF THIS SESSION

During this session, you will guide students to:
- Examine the life and faith of Mary;
- Discover what faith is and what it takes to live a life of faith;
- Implement a lifestyle of faith, learning to step out in faith in everyday life.

WARM UP

STEPPING OUT IN FAITH—
Activities to illustrate trust.

TEAM EFFORT— JUNIOR HIGH/ MIDDLE SCHOOL

WHAT IS FAITH ALL ABOUT, ANYWAY?—
Students discuss a case where faith doesn't seem to work.

TEAM EFFORT— HIGH SCHOOL

MARY AND JOSEPH: A PROFILE OF FAITH—
A role-play illustrating the faith of Mary and Joseph at the conception of Jesus.

IN THE WORD

THE ABCs OF FAITH—
A Bible study examining the incredible faith of Mary as she trusted God through the unusual and difficult circumstances of her life.

THINGS TO THINK ABOUT (OPTIONAL)

Questions to get students thinking and talking about faith.

PARENT PAGE

A tool to get the session into the home and allow parents and young people to discuss various statements about faith.

MARY:
ORDINARY
PERSON,
EXTRAORDINARY
FAITH

LEADER'S DEVOTIONAL

"On the third day a wedding took place at Cana in Galilee. Jesus' mother was there. When the wine was gone, Jesus' mother said to him, 'They have no more wine.' His mother said to the servants, 'Do whatever he tells you'" (John 2:1,3,5).

Mary is a hero for believers today. Who was this woman who was chosen to be the earthly mother of the son of God? These are the two aspects to Mary's position in Scripture: First, she was the mother of Jesus. Second, she was an example of faith.

I've never been a mom, but I do have one. Actually, I have three mothers including my stepmom and my mother-in-law. You may say I've been blessed three times over. Being a mother means a woman spends nine months watching her body bloat to what she considers astronomic proportions. After the gestation period (sounds like an intestinal condition, doesn't it?), a woman encounters life's most excruciating pain as she delivers an infant with a huge head who travels through a small opening in a short amount of time. From that joy-filled, pain-packed moment forward a mom's job is to lose her job. Mary was a mom who knew she was raising a child to be an adult. It takes faith to raise any child, let alone if He is the Savior.

Mary is an example of faith because she believed God and obediently raised His Son. Mary knew from the beginning she would not only release her child one day like every mother must do, but that she would watch her son suffer unbearably. Mary was warned by the prophet Simeon that people would violently speak and act against Jesus and that, for her, it would be like a sword piercing her soul (see Luke 2:34,35). Many mothers fear such cruel treatment of their child. Few, if any, receive a clear and accurate prophecy of its occurrence.

What was behind Mary's faith? She knew and believed God. Her son was who God said He was—the promised Messiah. How did that affect her life? When a problem came and the wine ran dry, Mary—a picture of faith—went to her son and told Him of the need: "They have no more." After the request was made, Mary exhibited the next great step of faith: She commissioned the servants to "do whatever Jesus says."

A person of faith, whether a mom, a dad or an adult youth worker trying to help moms and dads get children through adolescence, needs to emulate Mary. Take your need to Jesus. Then, do whatever Jesus says. Letting go and believing is a heroic act. Many moms manifest such heroic faith on a daily basis. (Written by Doug Webster)

"To nourish children and raise them against odds is in any time, any place, more valuable than to fix bolts in cars or design nuclear weapons."
—a French proverb

MARY: ORDINARY PERSON, EXTRAORDINARY FAITH

K EY VERSE

"Blessed is she who has believed that what the Lord has said to her will be accomplished!"
Luke 1:45

B IBLICAL BASIS

Matthew 1:18-25; 17:20,21; Luke 1:26-38; 45-56; 2:34,35; John 2:1,3,5; Romans 4:20,21;
Philippians 4:13; 2 Timothy 1:12; Hebrews 11:1; James 2:17

T HE BIG IDEA

God is looking for people of faith—ordinary people who will place themselves in the hands of
an extraordinary God.

W ARM UP (5-10 MINUTES)

STEPPING OUT IN FAITH

OPTION 1

• Divide students into pairs.
• Have one of the partners close his or her eyes, while the other partner leads him or her
around the inside or outside of the building. Caution those who do the leading that they are
responsible for their "blind" person's safety.
• Give each pair about three minutes for the first person to lead the other. After three minutes,
have the partners switch roles.
• When the six minutes are up, gather the group together to discuss the following questions:
1. How did you feel while being led around?
2. Was it difficult for you to keep your eyes closed and trust your partner? Why or why not?
3. Could you trust the person leading you around? Why or why not?
4. How does this exercise relate to trusting God and having faith in Him?

Fold

BELIEVING

1. What does verse 45 say about Mary's attitude about this announcement?

2. How do the following verses relate to Mary and her faith? Romans 4;20,21; Hebrews 11:1

3. What obstacles could have stood in the way of Mary believing the message from the angel?

4. How does Luke 1:46-55 reflect Mary's faith in God and His plan for her life?

COMMITMENT TO ACTION

1. From Matthew 1:18-25, how did Joseph react to the news?

2. How did Joseph show his faith?

3. How are faith and obedience related according to Philippians 4:13 and James 2:17?

To wrap up your time in the "In The Word" section, secure a copy of *Indiana Jones and the Last
Crusade* and show the scene where Indiana Jones is making his "step of faith" across the
chasm to where the Holy Grail is located. It's an excellent clip to show the need to step out in
obedience to demonstrate faith.

So WHAT?

Having a Moving Faith
"He replied, 'Because you have so little faith. I tell you the truth, if you had faith as small as a mustard seed, you can say
to this mountain, "Move from here to there" and it will move. Nothing will be impossible for you'" (Matthew 17:20,21).
1. What is a "mountain" that needs to be moved in your life?

2. How will you make yourself available to God in this situation?

3. What do you need to trust God for in this situation?

4. How can you act in obedience in this situation?

T HINGS TO THINK ABOUT (OPTIONAL)

• Use the questions on page 69 after or as a part of "In the Word."
1. What is faith?
   What does it mean to have faith in God?
2. What are some things that people place their faith in?
3. What are some of the roadblocks that keep us from having greater faith in God?

P ARENT PAGE

• Distribute page to parents.

OPTION 2

- Select at least two people from your group as volunteers. (More can be selected if time permits.) Send them out of the room.
- Set up the room that you are in as an obstacle course. (Use chairs, boxes, eggs or whatever you can think of.)
- Have the group split evenly on either side of the obstacle course. Assign one group to help guide the person successfully through the obstacle course and the other group to try to get the person to run into as many things as possible.
- Bring the first volunteer back into the room blindfolded. Explain that he or she is going to be walking through the obstacle course and that one group will be trying to help him or her and one group will be trying to distract him or her. After you have sent a few people through the course, discuss the following questions:

1. How did you feel while being directed through the obstacle course?
2. Who did you listen to and why? Did they mislead you or not?
3. Which group did you put your trust and faith in? Why?
4. How does this activity relate to trusting God and having faith in Him?

 **TEAM EFFORT—JUNIOR HIGH/MIDDLE SCHOOL** (15-20 MINUTES)

WHAT IS FAITH ALL ABOUT, ANYWAY?

- Read the following case study, or give each student a copy of "What Is Faith All About, Anyway?" on pages 63-64.
- Discuss the questions.

Sixteen-year-old Karen was lying in a coma in the community hospital. She had been in a horrible accident and was still on the critical list, but the doctors had not given up hope.

The same week that Karen was in the accident her church was having an evangelistic crusade. The guest speaker was an evangelist and faith healer. The pastor of the church and Karen's parents asked the faith healer to come to the hospital to pray that Karen's health might be restored. He agreed to try.

They all went to Karen's hospital room where she was literally being kept alive by a machine. The faith healer prayed and in an excited voice claimed that God had healed Karen.

Her parents were ecstatic and the pastor cried tears of joy. Karen remained in a coma. The faith healer insisted that she had been healed and that as a demonstration of faith they should ask the doctors to disconnect the life-support machine.

The doctors and nurses disagreed. Karen's parents went to court to get an order to force the hospital to disconnect the machine. Eventually Karen was taken off the machine at the insistence of the family and a court of law.

Karen died three days later.

1. What is your impression of this true story?
2. If you were Karen's parents or pastor, how would you feel?
3. Describe the faith of the following people:
   Karen's parents—
   Karen's pastor—
   The faith healer—
4. What would you say to the faith healer?
   What if he told Karen's parents that they just didn't have enough faith?
5. What does this story say about faith and trusting in God?

 **TEAM EFFORT—HIGH SCHOOL** (15-20 MINUTES)

MARY AND JOSEPH: A PROFILE OF FAITH

- Before the meeting (or the week before), select a group of five students to present a role-play of Matthew 1:18-25. Give them copies of "Mary and Joseph: A Profile of Faith" on page 65.
- After the presentation, discuss the questions.

Your group will act out Matthew 1:18-25. You'll need the following characters (in order of appearance):

Narrator
Mary
Joseph
Angel of the Lord
The prophet

If you can, use costuming. For added effect, you may want to get a little creative in how you present Matthew 1:18-25. Here are just a few ideas:

Act out the passage as a sequel to "Gone with the Wind."
Act out the passage as if it were happening on a daytime soap opera.
Act out the passage as if it were happening in today's culture.
Act out the passage from the viewpoint of a TV news report including film crews, news anchors and on-the-scene interviews.

After the role-play, discuss the following:
1. How did Mary and Joseph demonstrate that they were people of faith?
2. From this scene, how would you define the word "faith"?
3. When was a time that you had to have faith?
4. How would you describe faith to a person who is not a Christian?

 IN THE WORD (25-30 MINUTES)

THE ABCs OF FAITH

- Divide students into groups of three or four.
- Give each student a copy of "The ABCs of Faith" on pages 66-68 and a pen or pencil, or display a copy on an overhead projector.
- Have students complete the Bible study.

In all of the New Testament, one of the greatest portraits of faith is that of Mary. Mary had an incredible faith and trust in God—in what He said and what He wanted to do through her. God's desire is the same for us: He wants us to be people of faith.

AVAILABLITY
1. If you were Mary, how would you have reacted to the news from the angel?
   Read Luke 1:26-38,45-56.
2. How did Mary react in verses 34,38?
3. Faith is being open to what God wants to do in your life. In this passage, how was Mary open and available to God?

MARY:
ORDINARY
PERSON,
EXTRAORDINARY
FAITH

EAM EFFORT

WHAT IS FAITH ALL ABOUT, ANYWAY?

Sixteen-year-old Karen was lying in a coma in the community hospital. She had been in a horrible accident and was still on the critical list, but the doctors had not given up hope.

The same week that Karen was in the accident her church was having an evangelistic crusade. The guest speaker was an evangelist and faith healer. The pastor of the church and Karen's parents asked the faith healer to come to the hospital to pray that Karen's health might be restored. He agreed to try.

They all went to Karen's hospital room where she was literally being kept alive by a machine. The faith healer prayed and in an excited voice claimed that God had healed Karen.

Her parents were ecstatic and the pastor cried tears of joy. Karen remained in a coma. The faith healer insisted that she had been healed and that as a demonstration of faith they should ask the doctors to disconnect the life-support machine.

The doctors and nurses disagreed. Karen's parents went to court to get an order to force the hospital to disconnect the machine. Eventually Karen was taken off the machine at the insistence of the family and a court of law.

Karen died three days later.[1]

1. What is your impression of this true story?

_____

_____

_____

2. If you were Karen's parents or pastor, how would you feel?

_____

_____

_____

3. Describe the faith of the following people:

_____

_____

_____

Karen's parents—

_____

_____

_____

 © 1996 by Gospel Light. Permission to photocopy granted.

MARY:
ORDINARY
PERSON,
EXTRAORDINARY
FAITH

Karen's pastor—

....
....
....

The faith healer—

....
....
....

4. What would you say to the faith healer?

....
....
....

What if he told Karen's parents that they just didn't have enough faith?

....
....
....

5. What does this story say about faith and trusting in God?

....
....
....

Note: 1. Adapted from Jim Burns, *Youth Worker's Book of Case Studies* (Ventura, Calif.: Gospel Light) p. 50.

MARY:
ORDINARY
PERSON,
EXTRAORDINARY
FAITH

*T*EAM *E*FFORT

MARY AND JOSEPH: A PROFILE OF FAITH

Your group will act out Matthew 1:18-25. You'll need the following characters (in order of appearance):

> Narrator
>
> Mary
>
> Joseph
>
> Angel of the Lord
>
> The prophet

If you can, use costuming. For added effect, you may want to get a little creative in how you present Matthew 1:18-25. Here are just a few ideas:

> Act out the passage as a sequel to "Gone with the Wind."
>
> Act out the passage as if it were happening on a daytime soap opera.
>
> Act out the passage as if it were happening in today's culture.
>
> Act out the passage from the viewpoint of a TV news report including film crews, news anchors and on-the-scene interviews.

After the role-play, discuss the following:

1. How did Mary and Joseph demonstrate that they were people of faith?

2. From this scene, how would you define the word "faith"?

3. When was a time that you had to have faith?

4. How would you describe faith to a person who was not a Christian?

 © 1996 by Gospel Light. Permission to photocopy granted.

MARY:
ORDINARY
PERSON,
EXTRAORDINARY
FAITH

IN THE WORD

THE ABCs OF FAITH

In all of the New Testament, one of the greatest portraits of faith is that of Mary. Mary had an incredible faith and trust in God—in what He said and what He wanted to do through her. God's desire is the same for us: He wants us to be people of faith.

Read Luke 1:26-38,45-56.

Availability

1. If you were Mary, how would you have reacted to the news from the angel?

....

....

....

2. How did Mary react in verses 34,38?

....

....

....

3. Faith is being open to what God wants to do in your life. From the passage, how was Mary open and available to God?

....

....

....

Believing

1. What does verse 45 say about Mary's attitude to the announcement?

....

....

....

2. How do the following verses relate to Mary and her faith?

   Romans 4:20,21

....

....

....

© 1996 by Gospel Light. Permission to photocopy granted.

MARY:
ORDINARY
PERSON,
EXTRAORDINARY
FAITH

Hebrews 11:1

3. What obstacles could have stood in the way of Mary believing the message from the angel?

4. How does Luke 1:46-55 reflect Mary's faith in God and what He wanted to do in her life?

Commitment to Action

1. From Matthew 1:18-25, how did Joseph react to the news?

2. How did Joseph show his faith?

3. How are faith and obedience related according to Philippians 4:13 and James 2:17?

 © 1996 by Gospel Light. Permission to photocopy granted.

MARY: ORDINARY PERSON, EXTRAORDINARY FAITH

So What?

Having a Moving Faith

"He replied, 'Because you have so little faith. I tell you the truth, if you had faith as small as a mustard seed, you can say to this mountain, "Move from here to there" and it will move. Nothing will be impossible for you'" (Matthew 17:20,21).

1. What is a "mountain" that needs to be moved in your life?

2. How will you make yourself available to God in this situation?

3. What do you need to trust God for in this situation?

4. How can you act in obedience in this situation?

© 1996 by Gospel Light. Permission to photocopy granted.

Things to Think About ③

1. What is faith?

_____

_____

_____

What does it mean to have faith in God?

_____

_____

2. What are some things that people place their faith in?

_____

_____

_____

3. What are some of the roadblocks that keep us from having greater faith in God?

_____

_____

Read Mat. 17:20-21

4. What is a "mountain" that needs to be moved in your life?

 © 1996 by Gospel Light. Permission to photocopy granted.

MARY:
ORDINARY
PERSON,
EXTRAORDINARY
FAITH

PARENT PAGE

PUTTING YOUR FAITH TO THE TEST

God is calling us to be people of faith, but what does that mean? What does true faith look like?

Give each person a piece of paper and a pencil or pen. Have them write the numbers from one to nine down the side of the paper. Read each of the following statements aloud. For each statement, have each person write down on a piece of paper *T* for true or *F* for false. After all the statements have been read, go over them and discuss your answers as a family. Be sure to be open and listen to each person's opinion.

True or False?
1. It is impossible to have faith in something you can't see.
2. Seeing is believing.
3. You only believe as much as you live.
4. Faith is a blind trust in something you hope for.
5. Faith is more fact than feeling.
6. Faith without obedience is not really faith at all.
7. Unanswered prayer is a sign of a lack of faith.
8. Doubt is just a lack of faith.
9. Everybody has faith in something.

What Is Faith?
Read the following passages on faith. How does each passage describe faith?

Luke 1:45
Romans 4:20,21
Philippians 4:13
2 Timothy 1:12
Hebrews 11:1
James 2:17

1. When was a time you demonstrated faith in God?

_____

_____

_____

2. When was a time you demonstrated a lack of faith in God?

_____

_____

_____

© 1996 by Gospel Light. Permission to photocopy granted.

3. What issue in your life right now is one in which you need to exercise more faith?

....

....

....

4. What action steps can you take that will exercise your faith?

....

....

....

Take a moment to pray together as a family about the individual issues in each other's lives in which each of you needs to exercise more faith.

Session 4: "Mary: Ordinary Person, Extraordinary Faith" Date ....

 © 1996 by Gospel Light. Permission to photocopy granted.

THE HEART OF THE NEW TESTAMENT

LEADER'S PEP TALK

The day was October 17th. As my wife and I quietly slipped out of our room, we were praying that we wouldn't make a noise. Across the hallway and into the next room we crept. There he was, having one of the most significant days of his little life and didn't even know it. It was our son Joshua's first birthday. As we sang "Happy Birthday" to him, he looked at us as if we had lost our minds. It was his day, and we were going to go to his favorite place on earth—Disneyland!!! It was time for Joshua to experience his first ride at Disneyland. Joshua is a veteran of the park. He's seen everything and been almost everywhere in the park—but on a ride? Not until today.

As my wife and I entered the park with Joshua, we headed straight for the castle. Joshua's first ride? The Dumbo ride. After we climbed into the airborne elephant, I strapped us in. In moments, we were in the air going up, going down! I had a great time. Unfortunately for Joshua, it was another story. As his few strands of hair blew in the wind, his face became a picture of sheer panic!

That night after we laid Joshua in bed still clutching his Mickey Mouse balloon, my wife and I prayed for Joshua. We prayed that God would look over his little life and guide him. We prayed that God would reveal His love to Joshua and that Joshua would come to know Christ. We prayed that Joshua would know that Mom and Dad love him with all their hearts.

After we quietly crept out of his room, I went downstairs and sat in our living room. I pulled out my journal and began to write. I wrote Joshua a letter telling him how much I love him. I told him what he means to me, how my life will never be the same since God gave him to us as a gift. I told him of my prayers for him and what type of Dad I wanted to be for him. I wrote and I cried. I wrote and I poured my heart out to my son whom I love with all my heart. My prayer is that someday my son will open the pages of my journal and have a glimpse into his father's heart.

You know, in its purest form that's what the Bible is: God's love letter to the world letting us know how much He loves us. It's a glimpse into our Father's heart. The kids we work with need to see it, need to be exposed to it, need to be changed and moved by it. The students that we work with need to listen to their heavenly Father's heart as He pours out His love for them within the pages of His Word. I believe that one of the callings of the youth worker is to bring kids into contact with the living Word of God. It's a message from the Father's heart to ours. As you lead your students through the heart of the New Testament, listen carefully. The heartbeat you hear is your heavenly Father's.

THE INCREDIBLE, UNCONDITIONAL LOVE OF GOD

KEY VERSES

"For I am convinced that neither death nor life, neither angels nor demons, neither the present nor the future, nor any powers, neither height nor depth, nor anything else in all creation, will be able to separate us from the love of God that is in Christ Jesus our Lord."
Romans 8:38,39

BIBLICAL BASIS

Exodus 3:14;
Psalm 86:5;
Luke 15:11-24;
John 3:16,17; 8:1-11;
Romans 5:5-8; 8:38,39;
Ephesians 2:4-6;
1 John 3:1; 4:8-10

THE BIG IDEA

God has an incredible love for us—for everyone, any time, anywhere. God's love is not based on what you do but on who you are!

AIMS OF THIS SESSION

During this session, you will guide students to:
- Examine the amazing love God has for each of us;
- Discover how God's unconditional love can transform their lives;
- Implement an attitude of gratitude toward God based on a realization of how much He loves them.

WARM UP

WHAT DO YOU THINK?—
Students respond to statements about the love of God.

TEAM EFFORT— JUNIOR HIGH/ MIDDLE SCHOOL

BRIAN AND THE LOVE OF GOD—
Students discuss how to counsel a friend who questions the love of God.

TEAM EFFORT— HIGH SCHOOL

WHAT'S LOVE GOT TO DO WITH IT?—
An activity comparing God's standards of love and acceptance with the world's.

IN THE WORD

SNAPSHOTS OF LOVE—
A Bible study on the incredible, never-ending love of God.

THINGS TO THINK ABOUT (OPTIONAL)

Questions to get students thinking and talking about how they will respond to the love of God.

PARENT PAGE

A tool to get the session into the home and allow parents and young people to discuss how to live out God's love in their family life.

THE INCREDIBLE, UNCONDITIONAL LOVE OF GOD

LEADER'S DEVOTIONAL

"For God so loved the world, that he gave" (John 3:16).

"I love you." Three simple words define the unfathomable nature of God.

What can you, as an adult who has a love for God and a love for teenagers do to put the two together? You can teach, live, exemplify, recite, promise, model, proclaim, reach, pray, find and display the unconditional love of God. What does "I love you" really mean? Simply and profoundly stated: "I love you, period."

I states the personal nature of God's love for us. The personal pronoun I identifies God. When you use the word "I", you must be present, delivering the message personally. Let's say I tell you, "I've heard it said 'I love you' is a message God wants to give to you." The communiqué is valuable, but it puts an emphasis on my integrity, intelligence and insights. As much as I'd like to overrate all of the above three qualities in my life, wouldn't you rather hear it straight from the One that spoke the message in the first place? "I am Who I am" (Exodus 3:14) wants to tell you, "I love you."

Love is the verb—the action. God's incredible, unconditional love is not just an emotion. It's not a descriptive term. The love of God is an action. Young people need to see to believe. God's personal love is made real through powerful action.

You is the object of the statement. The active love of a personal God is given directly to you and to me. Young people are desperately searching for love. They pay to watch other people love each other in movies. They dial in to hear people sing about love in songs and music videos. Deep inside they wonder if they will ever experience exclusive love from someone else. That's why marriage continues to be a trendy institution. What kid doesn't want to be the object of the I-love-you message?

Finally, punctuate the I-love-you message with the period. The punctuation mark of God is the Cross. The death of Christ is the period at the end of God's "I love you." Paul says, "But God demonstrates his own love for us in this: While we were still sinners, Christ died for us" (Romans 5:8). The love of God is finalized in the cross of Jesus Christ. There are no *ifs, ands* or *buts* to this message of love. May God's message of His incredible, unconditional, personal, active love be the hallmark of your ministry. Kids are dying to hear it and God died to share it. (Written by Doug Webster)

"It is another's fault if he be ungrateful; but it is mine if I do not give."
—Seneca

THE INCREDIBLE, UNCONDITIONAL LOVE OF GOD

KEY VERSES

"For I am convinced that neither death nor life, neither angels nor demons, neither the present nor the future, nor any powers, neither height nor depth, nor anything else in all creation, will be able to separate us from the love of God that is in Christ Jesus our Lord." Romans 8:38,39

BIBLICAL BASIS

Exodus 3:14; Psalm 86:5; Luke 15:11-24; John 3:16,17; 8:1-11; Romans 5:5-8; 8:38,39; Ephesians 2:4-6; 1 John 3:1; 4:8-10

THE BIG IDEA

God has an incredible love for us—for everyone, anytime, anywhere. God's love is not based on what you do but on who you are!

WARM UP (5-10 Minutes)

WHAT DO YOU THINK?

• Hand out three signs to every person in the room—one with the word "Agree" written on it, one with the word "Undecided" and the third with the word "Disagree."
• Option: You could write the letters A, D and U in large block letters on 3x5-inch index cards for students to hold up. Tell them that A means "Agree," D means "Disagree" and U means "Undecided."
• Read the following statements and have the students hold up the sign with their responses.
• Have some from the "Agree" side share their reasons why they agreed and have some from the "Disagree" side share their reasons why they disagree.

1. God's love is based on what you do.
2. God's love is based purely on who you are.
3. God will love you more if you go to church and read the Bible regularly.

---- Fold ----

SNAPSHOT TWO: THE UNCONDITIONAL LOVE OF GOD

Read Luke 15:11-24.

1. What was the younger son's attitude?

2. What changed the younger son's attitude?

3. How did the father respond to his son coming home?

Was that the expected response?

4. How do you think the son felt about coming home?

About the reception he got?

5. How does this story reflect the unconditional love of God?

SNAPSHOT THREE: YOU AND THE LOVE OF GOD

Read John 3:16,17 and Romans 5:5-8.

1. How has God shown His love for you?

2. Why do you think God took the initiative in loving us and giving Jesus Christ's life for ours?

3. How does knowing the depth of God's love for you impact the way you see yourself and others?

4. What does Romans 8:38,39 mean to you?

SO WHAT?

1. Has there ever been a time when you felt like the woman caught in the act of adultery or the prodigal son and you wondered if God could ever love you after all that you've done? How did you feel?

2. In what area of your life do you need to experience more of the incredible, unconditional love of God?

Spend a couple of minutes and write a letter to God, telling Him how you feel about His love, your relationship with Him, and your gratitude and thankfulness to Him.

THINGS TO THINK ABOUT (OPTIONAL)

• Use the questions on page 83 after or as a part of "In the Word."

1. What makes a love that is based on who you are and not what you do so attractive?

2. What makes it so difficult to understand or accept the love of God?

3. Is there someone you know who needs to hear about the incredible, unconditional love of God? What will you do about it?

4. God's radical love for us calls for a response. How can you respond to God's love today?

PARENT PAGE

• Distribute page to parents.

4. If you love others, God will love you.
5. God loves Christians more than non-Christians.
6. I have had a time in my life when I felt there was no way that God could still love me.
7. I have a hard time feeling like God loves me.

 ## TEAM EFFORT—JUNIOR HIGH/MIDDLE SCHOOL (15-20 MINUTES)

BRIAN AND THE LOVE OF GOD

- Divide students into groups of three or four.
- Give each group a copy of "Brian and the Love of God" on pages 78-79 or display a copy using an overhead projector.
- Have the groups read the story and discuss the questions at the end of the story.

The bell rings just as you slip into your chair. As you pull your homework out of your book, you lean over to talk to Brian, one of your friends since fifth grade. He tells you that he needs to talk to you after class and that it's really important. As you lean back into your chair, you notice the expression on Brian's face—one of anger and frustration, yet one of being lost.

You and Brian have done everything together: vacations, church events, everything. But lately you've seen some changes. Brian's parents have been fighting more and more lately. In fact, Brian said they were yelling, fighting and throwing stuff a few weeks ago.

The bell rings and you head out of class with Brian close behind. As the two of you round the building going out toward the field, Brian opens up, "My parents are getting a divorce!"

"What!!! You've got to be kidding!" you exclaim.

"They told me before school today."

As you lean against the building, Brian starts to cry and says, "It's all I've thought about all day long. How could this have happened?! I thought my parents loved each other and now they're getting a divorce! Don't they even care about how I feel? Doesn't anyone care about how I feel? How could God let this happen? Doesn't He love us anymore? I pray for my parents, but why isn't God helping? Can't my parents see how much I hurt? Can't God see? Where is He when I need Him? Where is this God who supposedly loves me?"

1. What would you say to Brian?
2. How would you explain God's love to Brian?
3. Has there ever been a time when you felt that God didn't love you because of something that happened to you or that He couldn't possibly love you because of something you've done wrong? Explain.
4. What does Romans 8:38,39 say about God's love? How does this verse apply to Brian's situation?

 ## TEAM EFFORT—HIGH SCHOOL (15-20 MINUTES)

WHAT'S LOVE GOT TO DO WITH IT?

- Before your meeting, prepare four grocery-size paper bags with the following titles written in permanent markers on the outside of the bags:

Bag One	Beauty (looks, etc.)
Bag Two	Brains (intelligence, position, etc.)
Bag Three	Bucks (affluence, materialism, etc.)
Bag Four	Brawn (ability, performance, etc.)

- Fill each bag with objects that would represent those areas of our lives. (Be creative.) Below are some examples:

Beauty	mirror, make-up, clothes, weights, magazine covers
Brains	diploma, grades, business card, Wall Street Journal
Bucks	money, toy car, credit cards, jewelry, vacation guides, pictures of possessions
Brawn	sports equipment, trophies, awards, pictures of athletes and performers

- Divide your group into four fairly equal groups and give each group one of the bags. Explain that each bag represents an area that people use to gain value, acceptance and love. Explain that inside each bag are items that physically represent those areas. Write the following questions on the board or display them using an overhead projector and have each group go through the bag and answer them:

1. How does the world attach value to this particular area of life?
2. How does each item in your bag physically represent this area of life and the search for love and acceptance?
3. How and why do people seek after love and acceptance in these areas?
4. How does the world define love and acceptance?
5. How is God's love different from this world's version of love?

- When groups have finished, have them come back together and share a few of their items and their answers.

 ## IN THE WORD (25-30 MINUTES)

SNAPSHOTS OF LOVE

- Divide students into groups of three or four.
- Give each student a copy of "Snapshots of Love" on pages 80-82 and a pen or pencil, or display a copy on an overhead projector.
- Have students complete the Bible study.

God has an incredible, never-ending love for each of us. No matter who you are, where you've been or what you've done, one fact remains: God loves you! The following are three snapshots of God's love:

SNAPSHOT ONE: THE INCREDIBLE LOVE OF GOD
Read John 8:1-11.

1. Why was the woman brought to Jesus?

2. How did Jesus respond to those who brought her?

3. Jesus had every right to condemn the woman. How did Jesus respond to the woman?

(Tell students: Jesus treated her with respect and honor. The word "woman" is a word of respect and honor. It's the same word He used to address His mother while hanging on the cross.)

4. How do verses 10,11 reflect God's love?

THE INCREDIBLE, UNCONDITIONAL LOVE OF GOD

WARM UP

WHAT DO YOU THINK?

1. God's love is based on what you do.

2. God's love is based purely on who you are.

3. God will love you more if you go to church and read the Bible regularly.

4. If you love others, God will love you.

5. God loves Christians more than non-Christians.

6. I have had a time in my life when I felt there was no way that God could still love me.

7. I have a hard time feeling like God loves me.

© 1996 by Gospel Light. Permission to photocopy granted.

THE INCREDIBLE,
UNCONDITIONAL
LOVE OF GOD

TEAM EFFORT

BRIAN AND THE LOVE OF GOD

The bell rings just as you slip into your chair. As you pull your homework out of your book, you lean over to talk to Brian, one of your friends since fifth grade. He tells you that he needs to talk to you after class and that it's really important. As you lean back into your chair, you notice the expression on Brian's face—one of anger and frustration, yet one of being lost.

You and Brian have done everything together: vacations, church events, everything. Brian pretty much gets along with his parents. He has told you, "They're okay. We get into fights every once in a while, but for the most part we get along okay." But lately you've seen some changes. Brian's parents have been fighting more and more lately. In fact, Brian said they were yelling, fighting and throwing stuff a few weeks ago.

The bell rings and you head out of class with Brian close behind. As the two of you round the building going out toward the field, Brian opens up, "My parents are getting a divorce!"

"What!!! You've got to be kidding!" you exclaim.

"They told me before school today."

As you lean against the building, Brian starts to cry and says, "It's all I've thought about all day long. How could this have happened? I thought my parents loved each other and now they're getting a divorce! Don't they even care about how I feel? Doesn't anyone care about how I feel? How could God let this happen? Doesn't He love us anymore? I pray for my parents, but why isn't God helping? Can't my parents see how much I hurt? Can't God see? Where is He when I need Him? Where is this God who supposedly loves me?"

1. What would you say to Brian?

....
....
....

2. How would you explain God's love to Brian?

....
....
....

3. Has there ever been a time when you felt that God didn't love you because of something that happened to you or that He couldn't possibly love you because of something you've done wrong? Explain.

....
....
....

© 1996 by Gospel Light. Permission to photocopy granted.

4. What does Romans 8:38,39 say about God's love?

....

....

....

How does this verse apply to Brian's situation?

....

....

....

 © 1996 by Gospel Light. Permission to photocopy granted.

THE INCREDIBLE,
UNCONDITIONAL
LOVE OF GOD

SNAPSHOTS OF LOVE

God has an incredible, never-ending love for each of us. No matter who you are—no matter where you've been or what you've done one fact remains: God loves you! The following are three snapshots of God's love:

Snapshot One: The Incredible Love of God
Read John 8:1-11.

1. Why was the woman brought to Jesus?

_____

_____

_____

2. How did Jesus respond to those who brought her?

_____

_____

_____

3. Jesus had every right to condemn the woman. How did Jesus respond to the woman?

_____

_____

_____

4. How do verses 10 and 11 reflect God's love?

_____

_____

_____

Snapshot Two: The Unconditional Love of God
Read Luke 15:11-24.

1. What was the younger son's attitude?

_____

_____

_____

© 1996 by Gospel Light. Permission to photocopy granted.

2. What changed the younger son's attitude?

_____

_____

3. How did the father respond to his son coming home?

_____

_____

Was that the expected response?

_____

_____

4. How do you think the son felt about coming home?

_____

_____

About the reception he got?

_____

_____

5. How does this story reflect the unconditional love of God?

_____

_____

Snapshot Three: You and the Love of God

Read John 3:16,17 and Romans 5:5-8.

1. How has God shown His love for you?

_____

_____

© 1996 by Gospel Light. Permission to photocopy granted.

THE INCREDIBLE,
UNCONDITIONAL
LOVE OF GOD

2. Why do you think God took the initiative in loving us and giving Jesus Christ's life for ours?

3. How does knowing the depth of God's love for you impact the way you see yourself and others?

4. What does Romans 8:38,39 mean to you?

So What?

1. Has there ever been a time when you felt like the woman caught in the act of adultery or the prodigal son and you wondered if God could ever love you after all that you've done? How did you feel?

2. In what area of your life do you need to experience more of the incredible, unconditional love of God?

Spend a couple of minutes and write a letter to God, telling Him how you feel about His love, your relationship with Him and your gratitude and thankfulness to Him.

Dear God,

Love Always,

THE INCREDIBLE,
UNCONDITIONAL
LOVE OF GOD

ⓉHINGS TO THINK ABOUT

1. What makes a love that is based on who you are and not what you do so attractive?

2. What makes it so difficult to understand or accept the love of God?

3. Is there someone you know who needs to know about the incredible, unconditional love of God? What will you do about it?

4. God's radical love for us calls for a response. How can you respond to God's love today?

 © 1996 by Gospel Light. Permission to photocopy granted.

THE INCREDIBLE,
UNCONDITIONAL
LOVE OF GOD

PARENT PAGE

LOVE IS:

God has an incredible, unconditional love for every one of us. No matter who you are, where you've been or what you've done, God is ready with His arms open wide to welcome you home. Yet understanding and accepting God's love can be one of the toughest things to do. Below are some passages about the incredible love God has for you. Read the passages and complete the statements.

Psalm 86:5   God's love is:

_____
_____
_____

John 3:16,17   God's love is:

_____
_____
_____

Romans 5:5-8   God's love is:

_____
_____
_____

Romans 8:38,39   God's love is:

_____
_____
_____

Ephesians 2:4-6   God's love is:

_____
_____
_____

1 John 3:1   God's love is:

_____
_____
_____

1 John 4:8-10   God's love is:

_____
_____
_____

© 1996 by Gospel Light. Permission to photocopy granted.

THE INCREDIBLE, UNCONDITIONAL LOVE OF GOD

1. How can our family better live out God's love to each other?

....

....

....

2. How can our family be a light for the love of God:

....

....

....

In our extended family?

....

....

In our work and/or school?

....

....

In our community?

....

....

In our church?

....

....

....

In ....?

....

....

....

Spend some time in prayer as a family, thanking God for His love and the characteristics of the love that He has for you and your family. Spend part of your time completing the following statement:

"I thank You, God, for Your love because…"

Session 5: "The Incredible, Unconditional Love of God" Date 4/4/06

 © 1996 by Gospel Light. Permission to photocopy granted.

THE AMAZING GRACE OF GOD

KEY VERSES

"For it is by grace you have been saved, through faith—and this not from yourselves, it is the gift of God—not by works, so that no man can boast. For we are God's workmanship, created in Christ Jesus to do good works, which God prepared in advance for us to do."
Ephesians 2:8-10

BIBLICAL BASIS

Romans 5:1-5,15,18-21;
Ephesians 2:1-10

THE BIG IDEA

Grace is an undeserved gift to you from God.

AIMS OF THIS SESSION

During this session you will guide students to:

- Examine the amazing grace that God has for each of us;
- Discover how that grace impacts their lives;
- Implement a life of grace and an attitude of thankfulness to God.

WARM UP

GIFT SURVEY—

Students interview each other about receiving gifts.

TEAM EFFORT— JUNIOR HIGH/ MIDDLE SCHOOL

A FREE GIFT—

An object lesson and discussion about undeserved gifts.

TEAM EFFORT— HIGH SCHOOL

COIN GIVEAWAY—

An activity to illustrate the free gift of God's grace.

IN THE WORD

THANKS GOD, I NEEDED THAT!—

A Bible study on the undeserved gift of the grace of God.

THINGS TO THINK ABOUT (OPTIONAL)

Questions to get students thinking and talking about God's unmerited favor.

PARENT PAGE

A tool to get the session into the home and allow parents and young people to discuss the gifts God has given their family "just because."

THE AMAZING
GRACE OF GOD

LEADER'S DEVOTIONAL

"But the gift is not like the trespass. For if the many died by the trespass of the one man, how much more did God's grace and the gift that came by the grace of the one man, Jesus Christ, overflow to the many!" (Romans 5:15).

My eighth-grade math teacher, Mr. Kim, began many of his classes with classical music. Not a single fourteen-year-old was about to admit a liking for Mr. Kim's choice of entertainment. When you're in junior high, culture goes as deep as the acceptance level of your peers.

I had a successful year in Mr. Kim's class. Math came easier for me than most students so I rose to the top of the class, but not without hard work. Nobody got off easy in Mr. Kim's class. At the end of the year, I was in line for the eighth grade math student-of-the-year award. I was delighted in spite of the ribbing from a few classmates.

Unfortunately, my laziness clouded my judgment. I decided I could miss out on a final class. I already bagged an A, the award was mine so I reasoned "Why bother with the last class?" As I sat out on the school lawn, I remember a classmate finding me and saying "Webster, Mr. Kim is looking for you. You're in trouble for ditching class." Well, I wasn't quite ditching, I just wasn't showing up for work I already finished.

Mr. Kim didn't buy my excuse. I remember him saying "Do you want to take your hard work and your award and throw it away in one day?"

Mr. Kim's track record was not laced with grace. He was a tough teacher. In my case, Mr. Kim extended forgiveness. I received the math award after all. My fly-the-coop swan song discredited an attitude in keeping with the award. Even though my grade was an A, students don't get awarded for skipping class. Mr. Kim's grace gave me something I didn't deserve—regardless of my "good" past. I went sour in a second when I chose to dishonor my teacher. He had every opportunity to debunk me.

God doesn't honor us for good work. He extends His award of life as His grace. Have you ever had a time when you received something you really didn't deserve? It's called grace. Kids today need grace and forgiveness even though they deserve to be dropped from the ceremony. I've yet to meet the perfect student. God, however, continues to bring us along with His love. He's the one standing in the audience applauding when our name is called just like Mr. Kim. Knowing that Mr. Kim knew I didn't deserve it, my gratitude for the award was deepened. (Written by Doug Webster)

**"If you judge people, you have no time to love them."
—Mother Teresa**

THE AMAZING GRACE OF GOD

KEY VERSES

"For it is by grace you have been saved, through faith—and this not from yourselves, it is the gift of God—not by works, so that no man can boast. For we are God's workmanship, created in Christ Jesus to do good works, which God prepared in advance for us to do." Ephesians 2:8-10

IBLICAL BASIS

Romans 5:1-5,15,18-21; Ephesians 2:1-10

THE BIG IDEA

Grace is an undeserved gift to you from God.

WARM UP (5-10 MINUTES)

Gift Survey

• Have students form pairs.
• Give each student a copy of "Gift Survey" on pages 91-92, or display a copy using an overhead projector.
• Students interview each other to find out about gifts they have received.

Describe:
1. The best gift you have ever received.
2. The most useless gift you have ever received.
3. The ugliest gift you have ever received.
4. The gift you always wanted but have never received.
5. The most expensive gift you have ever received.
6. The smallest gift you have ever received.
7. The strangest or funniest gift you have ever received.
8. The most meaningful gift you have ever received.

-------- Fold --------

So What?

1. What is one thing that has challenged or surprised you from this session on God's grace?

2. What is one area in which you need to experience more of God's grace?

HINGS TO THINK ABOUT (OPTIONAL)

• Use the questions on page 96 after or as a part of "In the Word."
1. From Ephesians 2:8, why did God do it all for us?
2. "Mercy is not getting what you do deserve. Grace is getting what you don't deserve." What does that statement mean?
   Why is it so difficult for us to understand and accept God's grace?
3. Who in your life needs to hear about the message of God's grace? What would you tell him or her?

PARENT PAGE

• Distribute page to parents.

A FREE GIFT

- Prepare a nicely wrapped box with something of some value inside ($10.00, a scholarship to a youth group event, or anything else you can think of). Make a big deal about the gift and say that you as the giver can give it to anyone you want to.
- Select a visitor or someone from your group. Ask them a few questions and give them the gift. Let them open the gift in front of the group.
- Discuss the following questions:

1. Did _____ deserve the gift?
2. (To the person) How did it feel to get a gift that you didn't deserve?
3. (To the group) How is this like God's grace to us?

- Divide the students into groups of two or three and give each group a piece of paper and a pen or pencil.
- Have each group come up with a list of the many undeserved gifts that God has given them.
- After three to five minutes, have the groups share their lists. Make a master list on a piece of posterboard, a chalkboard, a white board or an overhead projector.
- Discuss the following questions:

1. How do you feel after looking at that list?
2. Why do you think God has given us so much, even though we don't deserve it?
3. How would you explain the word "grace" to someone?

COIN GIVEAWAY

- Provide enough pennies or other coins so that everyone in your group can have two or three.
- Tell students that on the count of three their job is to give away as many coins as they can according to the following rules:

  They can only give away one at a time.

  They must take any coin given to them.

- Give them about two or three minutes to give away as many coins as they can.
- After the allotted time is up, discuss the following questions:

1. How did you feel when you gave away money?
2. How did it feel to receive money?
3. What are some things that God has given you by His grace? (Just because He loves you—even though you don't deserve it!)
4. How would you explain the word "grace" to someone?

Fold

THANKS GOD, I NEEDED THAT!

- Divide students into groups of three or four.
- Give each student a copy of "Thanks God, I Needed That!" on pages 93-95 and a pen or pencil, or display a copy on an overhead projector.
- Have students complete the Bible study.

God's grace is amazing because it's free. God gives us grace not because we deserve it but because of His love for us. God is a God of grace, giving us that which we don't deserve.

Read Ephesians 2:1-10.

GRACE IS A GIFT OF LIFE (vv. 1-3,5)
1. According to verses 1-3, what were we dead in?

....

2. How does verse 5 reflect God's grace?

....

3. What are we alive to now (see Romans 5:1-5; 18-21)?

....

GRACE IS A GIFT OF LOVE (v. 4)
1. According to verse 4, where does God's mercy and grace for us come from?

....

2. What are some words that describe the love of God?

....

3. How does it feel to know that you are loved by your Creator no matter who you are or what you've done?

....

GRACE IS A GIFT OF SALVATION (vv. 5-9)
1. What do you think it means to be saved by grace?

....

2. From verses 5-9, what has God done for you by grace?

....

3. Why does God save us by grace through faith?

....

4. What are some ways people try to attain salvation?

....

GRACE IS A GIFT OF A FUTURE (v. 10)
1. What do you think it means to be God's workmanship?

....

2. What is it that "God [has] prepared in advance for us to do"?

....

3. How does it feel to know that God believes in your future and has taken time to plan it?

....

4. How does verse 10 reflect the grace of God?

....

WARM UP

GIFT SURVEY

Describe:

1. The best gift you have ever received.

....
....
....

2. The most useless gift you have ever received.

....
....
....

3. The ugliest gift you have ever received.

....
....
....

4. The gift you always wanted but have never received.

....
....
....

5. The most expensive gift you have ever received.

....
....
....

6. The smallest gift you have ever received.

....
....
....

 © 1996 by Gospel Light. Permission to photocopy granted.

THE AMAZING
GRACE OF GOD

7. The strangest or funniest gift you have ever received.

....
....
....

8. The most meaningful gift you have ever received.

....
....
....

 **IN THE WORD**

THANKS GOD, I NEEDED THAT!

God's grace is amazing because it's free. God gives us grace, not because we deserve it, but because of His love for us. God is a God of grace, giving that which we don't deserve.

Read Ephesians 2:1-10.

Grace Is a Gift of Life (vv. 1-3,5)

1. According to verses 1-3, what were we dead in?

2. How does verse 5 reflect God's grace?

3. What are we alive to now? (See Romans 5:1-5; 18-21.)

Grace Is a Gift of Love (v. 4)

1. According to verse 4, where does God's mercy and grace for us come from?

2. What are some words that describe the love of God?

3. How does it feel to know that you are loved by your Creator no matter who you are or what you've done?

 © 1996 by Gospel Light. Permission to photocopy granted.

THE AMAZING GRACE OF GOD

Grace Is a Gift of Salvation (vv. 5-9)

1. What do you think it means to be saved by grace?

_____

_____

_____

2. From verses 5-9, what has God done for you by grace?

_____

_____

_____

3. Why does God save us by grace through faith?

_____

_____

_____

4. What are some ways people try to attain salvation?

_____

_____

_____

Grace Is a Gift of a Future (v. 10)

1. What do you think it means to be God's workmanship?

_____

_____

_____

2. What is it that "God [has] prepared in advance for us to do"?

_____

_____

_____

3. How does it feel to know that God believes in your future and has taken time to plan it?

_____

_____

_____

© 1996 by Gospel Light. Permission to photocopy granted.

4. How does verse 10 reflect the grace of God?

....

....

....

So What?

1. What is one thing that has challenged or surprised you from this session on God's grace?

....

....

....

2. What is one area in which you need to experience more of God's grace?

....

....

....

 © 1996 by Gospel Light. Permission to photocopy granted.

**THE AMAZING
GRACE OF GOD**

Things to Think About

1. From Ephesians 2:8, why did God do it all for us?

   ....

   ....

   ....

2. "Mercy is not getting what you do deserve. Grace is getting what you don't deserve." What does that statement mean?

   ....

   ....

   ....

   Why is it so difficult for us to understand and accept God's grace?

   ....

   ....

   ....

3. Who in your life needs to hear about the message of God's grace? What would you tell him or her?

   ....

   ....

   ....

© 1996 by Gospel Light. Permission to photocopy granted.

**THE AMAZING
GRACE OF GOD**

GETTING WHAT YOU DON'T DESERVE

It was a cold, overcast day as I stood in front of Cell 21 in the basement of Barracks 11—the Death Block. What stood before me was a memorial to one of the most extraordinary people and events in all of Auschwitz—Father Maximilian Kolbe.

Father Maximilian Kolbe was a Catholic priest sentenced to be imprisoned in Auschwitz in May 1941. Upon his arrival at KL Auschwitz, he was informed that the life expectancy of a priest was about a month in Auschwitz. Father Kolbe took it upon himself to be an agent of love within the dismal hopelessness of the barbed wire fences.

One night in July 1941, amidst the sounds of motorcycles and barking dogs, a man from Barracks 14 escaped from Auschwitz. The next morning as the prisoners lined up for morning roll call, they noticed the gallows in front of them—empty. The escapee had succeeded, yet someone would pay the price for him. That morning, 10 men were selected to die in the starvation bunker inside the Death Block. One of those men was 5659. As the ten were being led away to screams of horror, a small, frail man stepped forward. His number was 16670. His name was Father Maximilian Kolbe.

"Sir, I'd like to die in place of one of those men."

"In whose place do you want to die?" asked the Commander.

"For that one." Father Kolbe lifted his finger and pointed at 5659. And in an instant, 5659 was erased off the death ledger and 16670 was entered. One life for another—a gift of life. On August 14, 1941, in a starvation bunker known only as Cell 21 in the basement of Barracks 11, one man gave the gift of life by dying in place of another. Number 16670 died in place of 5659.

As I peered through the bars into the starvation cell where Maximilian Kolbe died, I felt as if I were on holy ground. The plaque on the wall of the cell and the memorial fire in the center of the cell pointed to what was one of the most extraordinary events in the history of this place called Auschwitz. Here was light in the darkness, love afloat in the middle of a sea of hate, and hope in the midst of madness. As I stood at the place where one man gave his life for another in an act of love—the gift of life—I was broken and changed.

It was a cold, overcast day when another Man gave His life. He was Light in the darkness, Love afloat in the middle of a sea of hate, and Hope in the midst of madness. On that hill, Jesus gave His life for all humanity—not only for all humankind but more specifically for you and me. A gift of life and an act of love given because of God's incredible love for you and me.

Too often I lose sight of God's love and His grace. Too often I get so wrapped up in my busyness for Him, that I miss the opportunity to be with Him. Standing in front of that cell, I was brought face-to-face with the radical love that God has for you and for me. God loved you and me so much that He couldn't stand to live without us for eternity. It was a love that drove Him to action—a love that drove Jesus Christ to die on a cross for you and me. That's the message of the New Testament.

As I walked away from that moment in time at the starvation cell where Father Maximilian Kolbe gave his life for another, I wondered about 5659. Who was he? What went through his mind as he saw Father Kolbe being led away to his death, while he was given the gift of life?

 © 1996 by Gospel Light. Permission to photocopy granted.

THE AMAZING GRACE OF GOD

I walked away from the basement of Barracks 11 broken—and changed. Broken, that a man would give his life for another—changed in my gratitude for what was done for me on calvary. Just like 5659, I was being led away to my death when another Man stepped forward out of the crowd. Looking into my eyes, He saw the terror and the pain.

"Sir, I'd like to die in the place of one of those men," He said.

"In whose place do you want to die?"

"For that one."

Just as Father Maximilian Kolbe, 16670, gave the gift of life to prisoner 5659, so Jesus Christ has given us the gift of life and of grace. For just as prisoner 5659 experienced a radical grace—a gift that was never deserved—so do we experience a gift that we do not deserve: the amazing grace of God!

1. How does the story of Father Maximilian Kolbe illustrate the grace of God?

2. What are some things God has given or done for you or your family "just because" even though you didn't deserve it?

3. Read Romans 5 as a family and take some time to reflect and thank God for His grace and what He's given you—even though you don't deserve it!

Session 6: "The Amazing Grace of God"
Date

© 1996 by Gospel Light. Permission to photocopy granted.

BEING A PART OF GOD'S FAMILY—
FITTING INTO THE PUZZLE

KEY VERSE

"The body is a unit, though it is made up of many parts; and though all its parts are many, they form one body. So it is with Christ."
1 Corinthians 12:12

BIBLICAL BASIS

John 13:14,15;
Romans 12:4,5,10;
1 Corinthians 12:12-27;
Galatians 6:2;
Ephesians 2:19,20; 4:16;
Philippians 2:1-5;
Hebrews 10:24,25;
1 John 4:7,8; 3:16-18

THE BIG IDEA

When you become a Christian, you become a part of the Body of Christ—the family of God.

AIMS OF THIS SESSION

During this session you will guide students to:
• Examine what it means to be a part of the Body of Christ;
• Discover their own unique place and responsibility within the Body;
• Implement a decision and a plan to move into action to make a difference within the Body of Christ.

WARM UP

FAMILY PORTRAITS—
Students draw pictures depicting the Church, the Body of Christ.

TEAM EFFORT—
JUNIOR HIGH/
MIDDLE SCHOOL

BEING AN INGREDIENT FOR GOD—
Students compare the importance of their role in the Body of Christ to the importance of the ingredients in a recipe.

TEAM EFFORT—
HIGH SCHOOL

THE PUZZLE OF THE FAMILY OF GOD—
A comparison of how the individual members of the family of God are like the pieces to a puzzle—each one important to complete the whole.

IN THE WORD

THE BODY IN ACTION—
A Bible study on what our rights, responsibilities and attitudes should be as members of the Body of Christ.

THINGS TO THINK ABOUT (OPTIONAL)

Questions to get students thinking and talking about how to be effective members of the Body of Christ.

PARENT PAGE

A tool to get the session into the home and allow parents and students to discuss how to encourage every member to carry out his or her responsibilities and feel a part of the family.

BEING A PART OF GOD'S FAMILY—FITTING INTO THE PUZZLE

LEADER'S DEVOTIONAL

"In Christ we who are many form one body, and each member belongs to all the others" (Romans 12:5).

The National Football League finished its annual draft yesterday. The first round, top-five draft choices always draw big attention. These highly acclaimed and soon-to-be-well-paid college students are in a position to be the league's newest celebrities. The covers of sports pages across the nation will soon be pictorial and verbal trophies to these top kids. Virtually every time the new player and soon-to-be-star is picked, he is quickly issued a team jersey, team hat and number. Of course, the photo opportunity broadcasts the team as the victor of the spoils.

What would it be like if we, the Church, gave the same attention to welcoming new believers into the family of God? What if a new Christian received a party at the next church service? We would call her name, take pictures and speak clearly into the microphone for all to hear what a wonderful joy it is to have her on God's team. Churches would experience the incredible joy God has every time someone new is added to His family.

Funny, another sports tradition could be worked into the fabric of churches more readily than the draft celebration and that is the moment after a player is called for a foul or penalty. The referee states something like "Number 62: illegal use of hands on offense—10-yard penalty." Now there is a picture for the church. "Mr. John Doe, husband of Jane, father of Johnny and Joanie: illegal use of company funds—immediate dismissal from the job—continual sneers from church members behind his back—10-year penalty and recovery period."

In sports, the whole team suffers from a penalty. According to Paul's words in Romans, the whole Body of Christ belongs to each other, sharing in their pain and rejoicing in their success. According to what I see in many churches, when you go anywhere—up or down, you go alone even if you succeed. Why is it easier to desecrate a believer's sin than to celebrate a believer's salvation or success?

If we overlook God's Word, we miss the power of being a part of God's people. Christianity is not just a right relationship with God or a guarantee of going to heaven. According to Scripture, becoming a believer means stepping into God's family. When the disciples asked Jesus to teach them how to talk to God, He said to pray like this: "Our Father" and He remained in the third person using words like "us," "we" and "our." God has always and will always look at us as a family in faith with one Father. (Written by Doug Webster)

> "One truly affectionate soul in a family will exert a sweetening and harmonizing influence upon all its members."
> —Henry Van Dyke

BEING A PART OF GOD'S FAMILY— FITTING INTO THE PUZZLE

Key Verse

"The body is a unit, though it is made up of many parts; and though all its parts are many, they form one body. So it is with Christ." 1 Corinthians 12:12

Biblical Basis

John 13:14,15; Romans 12:4,5,10; 1 Corinthians 12:12-27; Galatians 6:2; Ephesians 2:19,20; 4:16; Philippians 2:1-5; Hebrews 10:24,25; 1 John 4:7,8; 3:16-18

The Big Idea

When you become a Christian, you become a part of the Body of Christ—the family of God.

Warm Up (5-10 Minutes)

Family Portraits

- Give each student a piece of paper and a pen or pencil. On one side of the paper have them draw a picture that represents the Church/family of God.
- After they have drawn the pictures, either have each person share what his or her picture depicts, or have them get into groups of three or four and share about their pictures. Discuss the following questions:
  1. How is the Church like a family?
  2. How is our youth group like a family?

Team Effort—Junior High/Middle School (15-20 Minutes)

Being an Ingredient for God

- Prior to your meeting, buy a chocolate cake or chocolate chip cookies and the following items: flour, sugar, eggs, chocolate chips or cocoa, milk, butter and baking powder.
- Display the above ingredients in bowls, along with the cake or cookies. Explain to your group that you have the ingredients needed to make a chocolate cake or chocolate chip

---

Fold

So What?

1. What can you do to help people feel like they belong?

....

2. What are some roles that you can fill in our group to make it be more of a family?

3. What can we do to care more for others in our group?

What will you do personally to care more for others in our group?

....

Things to Think About (optional)

- Use the questions on page 106 after or as a part of "In the Word."
  1. What area of giftedness do you see yourself adding to the Body of Christ?
  2. What keeps us from reaching out to others who are in need?
  3. What keeps you from reaching out to others?
  4. What are some things which make you feel like you...

Belong?
Are needed?
Are cared for?

Parent Page

- Distribute page to parents.

cookies and the final product. Read 1 Corinthians 12:12 and explain that just as there are many different elements or parts in the body, to make a cake you also need different ingredients.

• Invite students to sample the individual ingredients, describing how they taste. Then have the students sample the final product, describing how it tastes. Discuss the following questions:

1. **How does this illustrate what it means to be a part of the family of God?**
2. **What would happen if we forgot one or more of the ingredients?**
3. **How important are each of the ingredients?**
4. **What do you feel is your part (ingredient) in the family of God?**
5. **What are some of the advantages of being an active part the family of God?**

TEAM EFFORT—HIGH SCHOOL (15-20 MINUTES)

THE PUZZLE OF THE FAMILY OF GOD

• Buy or borrow a small child's puzzle (with approximately 12 pieces).
• Hand out the puzzle pieces to volunteers (one piece per volunteer).
• Ask each student to describe in detail from that one piece what the picture of the puzzle is.
• Then have the group of volunteers come together and build the puzzle.
• Discuss the questions which follow.
• Option: At the end of the lesson, give each person in the whole group a piece of another puzzle to symbolize that he or she belongs to the group and to God's puzzle—the Body of Christ.

1. **What are some similarities between the puzzle and being a part of the family of God?**

Possible answers:
• Each piece is needed to make the picture complete. We are all needed in the family of God to complete God's design.
• Each piece is not independent from the others. We are not independent from each other; we need each other to help each of us find our place and to work together to complete the picture—God's plan.
• Without every piece the puzzle is incomplete. Each person is essential and valuable in the Body of Christ.

2. **What are some other items that are like a puzzle which can represent an aspect of the Body of Christ?**

Possible answers:
• Tools (each has a different and unique use);
• Keys (each one is unique and opens different doors);
• Sports team (each person on the team has a different role, position or responsibility on the team).

3. **Is being a part of a church necessary to a Christian? Why or why not?**

4. **What are the advantages of being plugged into the family of God?**

Fold

IN THE WORD (25-30 MINUTES)

THE BODY IN ACTION

• Divide students into groups of three or four.
• Give each student a copy of "The Body in Action" on pages 103-105 and a pen or pencil, or display a copy on an overhead projector.
• Have students complete the Bible study.

Read 1 Corinthians 12:12-27. What does the passage say about being a part of the Body?

EVERYBODY BELONGS (vv. 12-20)

1. What are some things that keep people from feeling like they belong to a group?

2. What are some words that describe how you feel when you belong?

3. What does verse 18 mean for our group and for you personally?

4. Why did God give different roles to people in the family of God?

EVERYBODY IS NEEDED (vv. 21-24)

1. Why is every part needed in the Body?

2. Part of being needed in the Body is having a responsibility to one another. From the following passages, what are some of our responsibilities to one another? Also, how does that apply in real life?

John 13:14,15

Romans 12:4,5,10

Galatians 6:2

Ephesians 4:16

Philippians 2:1-5

Hebrews 10:24,25

1 John 4:7,8

EVERYBODY IS CARED FOR (vv. 25-27)

1. From vv. 25-27, what should our attitude be toward others in the family of God?

2. Read 1 John 3:16-18. We are called to love in deed and truth, not merely in words. What are some things that you can do to put love into action and care for those around you?

IN THE WORD

THE BODY IN ACTION

Read 1 Corinthians 12:12-27. What does the passage say about being a part of the Body?

....

....

....

Everybody Belongs (vv. 12-20)

1. What are some things that keep people from feeling like they belong to a group?

    ....

    ....

    ....

2. What are some words that describe how you feel when you belong?

    ....

    ....

    ....

3. What does verse 18 mean for our group and for you personally?

    ....

    ....

    ....

4. Why did God give different roles to people in the family of God?

    ....

    ....

    ....

Everybody Is Needed (vv. 21-24)

1. Why is every part needed in the Body?

    ....

    ....

    ....

 © 1996 by Gospel Light. Permission to photocopy granted.

2. Part of being needed in the Body is having a responsibility to one another. From the following passages, what are some of our responsibilities to one another? Also, how does that apply in real life?

....

....

John 13:14,15

....

....

Romans 12:4,5,10

....

....

Galatians 6:2

....

....

Ephesians 4:16

....

....

Philippians 2:1-5

....

....

Hebrews 10:24,25

....

....

....

© 1996 by Gospel Light. Permission to photocopy granted.

1 John 4:7,8

....
....
....

Everybody Is Cared For (vv. 25-27)

1. From vs. 25-27, what should our attitude be toward others in the family of God?

....
....
....

2. Read 1 John 3:16-18. We are called to love in deed and truth, not merely in words. What are some things that you can do to put love into action and care for those around you?

....
....

So What?

1. What can you do to help people feel like they belong?

....
....
....

2. What are some roles that you can fill in our group to make it be more of a family?

....
....
....

3. What can we do to care more for others in our group?

....
....
....

What will you do personally to care more for others in our group?

....
....
....

 © 1996 by Gospel Light. Permission to photocopy granted.

BEING A
PART OF GOD'S
FAMILY—FITTING
INTO THE PUZZLE

Things to Think About

1. What area of giftedness do you see yourself adding to the Body of Christ?

....

....

....

2. What keeps us from reaching out to others who are in need?

....

....

....

3. What keeps you from reaching out to others?

....

....

....

4. What are some things which make you feel like you...

....

....

....

Belong?

....

....

....

Are needed?

....

....

....

Are cared for?

....

....

....

**BEING A
PART OF GOD'S
FAMILY—FITTING
INTO THE PUZZLE**

PARENT PAGE

FAMILY BODY LIFE

Read 1 Corinthians 12:12-27 together as a family.

When we become Christians, we become a part of the Body of Christ—the family of God. As a part of God's family, we have a responsibility to accept, love and care for one another. The Body of Christ is like a family. Just as in the family of God the family members need to feel like they belong, that they have unique parts or responsibilities and need to feel that others care about them. Below is an inventory and discussion questions for your family to help you examine the essential areas of being a family.

On a scale of 1 to 10, have each person in your family rate your family on the following areas (1 = needs a major overhaul, and 10 = running like a champ):

Everybody belongs (everyone is of equal value).

1   2   3   4   5   6   7   8   9   10

Everybody is needed (everyone has a unique part or responsibility).

1   2   3   4   5   6   7   8   9   10

Everybody is cared for (everyone has their needs met).

1   2   3   4   5   6   7   8   9   10

1. What can we do as a family to make sure that everyone is of equal value?

....

....

....

2. What can we do in our family to make each person feels more a part of it?

....

....

....

3. What can we do as a family to make sure that each person has a vital and unique responsibility or role in our family?

....

....

....

4. What can we do to care more effectively for each person in our family?

....

....

....

 © 1996 by Gospel Light. Permission to photocopy granted.

BEING A PART OF GOD'S FAMILY—FITTING INTO THE PUZZLE

5. In which of the three areas—belonging, being needed, being cared for—are we doing well as a family?

_____

_____

_____

Which of the three areas do we need to improve?

_____

_____

_____

6. What are three action steps that we will take?

Action Step	When

7. A big part of being in the family of God is encouraging each other spiritually. What does our family do now to encourage spiritual growth in each other?

_____

_____

_____

What else can we do in the future to encourage each other to grow?

_____

_____

_____

"Consequently, you are no longer foreigners and aliens, but fellow citizens with God's people and members of God's household, built on the foundation of the apostles and prophets, with Christ Jesus himself as the chief cornerstone" (Ephesians 2:19,20).

Session 7: "Being a Part of God's Family—Fitting into the Puzzle"
Date _____

© 1996 by Gospel Light. Permission to photocopy granted.

BEING AN AGENT OF CHANGE— MAKING A KINGDOM IMPACT

KEY VERSE

"The King will reply, 'I tell you the truth, whatever you did for one of the least of these brothers of mine, you did it for me.'" Matthew 25:40

BIBLICAL BASIS

Matthew 13:33; 25:31-46;
2 Corinthians 5:17-20;
Philippians 4:13;
1 Thessalonians 2:8;
1 John 3:16-18

THE BIG IDEA

Being a Christian means being a part of God's plan to touch the world with His love.

AIMS OF THIS SESSION

During this session you will guide students to:
- Examine the heart of God for the lost and hurting of this world;
- Discover their role in God's plan to touch the world with His love;
- Implement a practical decision to become an agent of love and change.

WARM UP

PAPER CHARADES—
Students draw key session words.

TEAM EFFORT— JUNIOR HIGH/ MIDDLE SCHOOL

THE SHEEP AND GOATS PLAYERS—
Students act out the parable of the sheep and goats.

TEAM EFFORT— HIGH SCHOOL

SO WHERE'S GOD IN ALL OF THIS?—
Students contemplate a story about God's presence in the inner city.

IN THE WORD

MAKING A KINGDOM IMPACT—
A Bible study on the call of Christ to be an agent of change in the world.

THINGS TO THINK ABOUT (OPTIONAL)

Questions to get students thinking and talking about how they can make a difference in their world.

PARENT PAGE

A tool to get the session into the home and allow parents and young people to discuss how to be God's agents of change as a family.

BEING AN AGENT OF CHANGE— MAKING A KINGDOM IMPACT

LEADER'S DEVOTIONAL

"The kingdom of heaven is like yeast that a woman took and mixed into a large amount of flour until it worked all through the dough" (Matthew 13:33).

In God's economy, quantity is insignificant. Jesus' parable of the leavening bread told of a woman who added yeast to a large batch of bread dough. The power of the yeast in the dough causes a dynamic result. Just as a mustard-seed faith makes a tree-size impact in God's plan, so does an insignificant human who combines a little faith with a big batch of God in a starving world.

Another husband-and-wife team joined my wife and I on a mission trip to Haiti. He thoroughly enjoyed it, but she thoroughly hated it. Especially the time when we took rickety old rowboats across a large bay to a small fishing village called Labadie. The oarsmen were friendly, the view was beautiful and the water was a vibrant turquoise. As far as the wife was concerned the bay was too deep and the boats too old and frail. I could hear her voice calling from the boat behind us. Her husband did the best he could to comfort her while at the same time eating up the "Indiana Jones" nature of the trip. However, the rowboat excursion suffered in comparison to the flight back across the small island of Haiti on a tiny, nine-passenger aircraft. The drafty nature of a mountain-covered island provided quite an eventful ride. I must admit, I was a little squeamish and rather grateful to touch down safely at the Port-au-Prince airport.

What I admired most about the wife though was her willingness to go in spite of very strong reservations. She had no faith in old boats and small planes, but her little bit of faith in a big God made the event a success. Her life since then has been one of steady growth in impact for the kingdom of God. This mild-mannered woman and her husband launched a ministry in Eastern Europe. Not only is she raising kids there, she has also given birth to one there to boot. Their impact on thousands of lives, including many Eastern European teenagers, is an inspiration to me and an ongoing reminder of God's way of doing things. He doesn't need well-baked believers doing great things for Him. God will take a pinch of this or a seed of that and make a kingdom impact. (Written by Doug Webster)

**"Every morning lean thine arms awhile upon the windowsill of Heaven and gaze upon the Lord. Then, with that vision in thine heart, turn strong to meet the day."
—Anonymous**

BEING AN AGENT OF CHANGE – MAKING A KINGDOM IMPACT

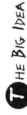 KEY VERSE

"The King will reply, 'I tell you the truth, whatever you did for one of the least of these brothers of mine, you did it for me.'" Matthew 25:40

 BIBLICAL BASIS

Matthew 13:33; 25:31-46; 2 Corinthians 5:17-20; Philippians 4:13; 1 Thessalonians 2:8; 1 John 3:16-18

THE BIG IDEA

Being a Christian means being a part of God's plan to touch the world with His love.

WARM UP (5-10 MINUTES)

PAPER CHARADES

- Divide the students into two groups. Give each group a few pieces of newsprint and a pencil.
- Have each group select an "artist" to illustrate each word. Have the artists come up to you and you whisper the word to be drawn to them. The first team to guess the picture correctly wins. Continue with other words.
- Use the following words: "world," "kingdom," "sheep," "serving" and "impact."

TEAM EFFORT—JUNIOR HIGH/MIDDLE SCHOOL (15-20 MINUTES)

THE SHEEP AND THE GOATS PLAYERS

- Select six students from your group and assign the following parts:

  2 sheep
  2 goats

Fold

---

iii

So WHAT?

1. What keeps you from being sensitive to the needs of those around you?

   What specific things can you do to be more sensitive to those in need?

2. Who in your life has the "face of Jesus"? What is God calling you to do in this person's life?

3. The sheep served God with what they had and who they were. What are some simple ways that you can serve God with who you are and the gifts He has given you?

4. What are three action steps that you will take to make a kingdom difference?

   Action Step One:

   Action Step Two:

   Action Step Three:

THINGS TO THINK ABOUT (OPTIONAL)

- Use the questions on page 118 after or as a part of "In the Word."

1. What are some things that you can do to make a difference in...
   Your Church?
   Your Home?
   Your School?
   Your Community?

2. Read Philippians 4:13. If you could be involved in making an impact for God in any way, what would you do? What's keeping you from doing that?

3. What do you think about the statement "Making a difference takes ordinary people doing ordinary things through the power of an extraordinary God?"

PARENT PAGE

- Distribute page to parents.

A person in need (who will act out *all* of the "needs")

Jesus

- Tell the players that as you read the story of the sheep and the goats, they will spontaneously act out the scene for the audience. Let them know that they need to really ham it up for effect. Give the players an opportunity to read Matthew 25:36-41 before acting it out so they know what to expect.
- Read Matthew 25:36-41 making sure to stop to let the players act out their individual parts.
- Hand out an old trophy (which you can get at a thrift store) as an Academy Award for the best performance of the group. You can also make up other categories for awards as well.

TEAM EFFORT—HIGH SCHOOL (15-20 MINUTES)

SO WHERE'S GOD IN ALL THIS?

- Divide students into groups of three or four.
- Give each group a copy of "So Where's God in All This?" on pages 113-114.
- Have students read the story and discuss the questions.
- Option: Read the account to the whole group and discuss the questions at the end.

They knew that they were in for a tough weekend when they had to step over the body of a drunk man to get into the hotel. Here they were in a rundown hotel a block from skid row in Los Angeles. The team was here for a weekend of ministry and changing lives—little did they know that the lives that would be changed were their own.

That night they were to tour the city—to allow God to break their hearts and to pray for the needs of the city. As they climbed into the blue Dodge van for the drive, the host asked this question, "Tonight, as you're looking around, answer these questions: Where is God in all this? If God is a God of love, then why does He allow the things to happen that you're going to see tonight? Where is He and why does He seem to be silent?"

As they drove the streets of inner-city Los Angeles, each one was affected by the scenes that they saw: the homeless women and children, drug deals, prostitutes (female *and* male) and fire barrels lit to provide some kind of warmth. As the van turned a corner, there in the dim street light a prostitute was making a score and getting into a Jeep Cherokee—off to some unknown destination. During all of this time the questions kept ringing in their ears: "Where is God in all this? Why does He seem to be silent?"

As the van arrived back at the hotel, the group shuffled into a small room off of the lobby, all the while pondering the questions. The room was uncomfortably quiet as they struggled with their emotions, trying to find some answer to the questions that were posed to them. One by one, students offered their opinions and thoughts; then it came back to the host, "Where was God tonight? Was He silent? I'll tell you where God was tonight: He was riding in a blue Dodge van. The question is not where is God in all this and does He care—the question is where are God's people who are called by His name, and do they really care enough to get involved in touching the world with His love?"

1. What did the host mean when he said "God was riding in a blue Dodge van"?
2. If you had been in that van, how would you have answered the question?
3. Do you see any situations around you where God seems to be silent?
4. Read 2 Corinthians 5:18-20 as a group. How do these verses relate to the story?
   What does it mean to be His ambassadors?

Fold

IN THE WORD (25-30 MINUTES)

MAKING A KINGDOM IMPACT

- Divide students into groups of three or four.
- Give each student a copy of "Making a Kingdom Impact" on pages 115-117 and a pen or pencil, or display a copy on an overhead projector.
- Have students complete the Bible study.

The call of Christ is a call to be an agent of change. God's desire is that we reach out to those around us and make a kingdom impact one life at a time.

Read Matthew 25:31-46.

1. List all the similarities and differences between the sheep and the goats.

Similarities	Differences

2. How are we like the sheep in the story?

How are we like the goats in the story?

BEING SENSITIVE TO THE NEEDS OF OTHERS

1. What is the difference between the attitude of the sheep in verse 37 and the goats in verse 44?

2. What keeps us from being sensitive to the needs of those around us?

SEEING THE FACE OF JESUS ON THOSE IN NEED

1. Who were the sheep really serving in verse 40?

2. What do you think about the statement "When you're serving those around you, you are really serving Jesus Christ"?

3. Why do you think the goats never saw the face of Jesus in the needy ones around them?

SERVING WITH WHAT YOU HAVE AND WHO YOU ARE

1. What are some of the ways the sheep ministered to those around them?

2. Why do you think the sheep were so surprised by the King's comment in verses 34-37?

3. What do you think Jesus is calling us to do in verse 40?

So many times we think that God is looking for the talented when in reality He is looking for the willing and available. God is looking for people who want to serve in the small things, in the "whatevers." Making a difference takes ordinary people doing ordinary things through the power of an extraordinary God.

TEAM EFFORT

SO WHERE'S GOD IN ALL THIS?

They knew that they were in for a tough weekend when they had to step over the body of a drunk man to get into the hotel. Here they were in a rundown hotel a block from skid row in Los Angeles. As they entered the hotel, a stale, smoky smell greeted them. The team was here for a weekend of ministry and changing lives—little did they know that the lives that would be changed were their own.

That night they were to tour the city—to allow God to break their hearts and to pray for the needs of the city. As they climbed into the blue Dodge van for the drive, the host asked this question, "Tonight, as you're looking around, answer these questions: Where is God in all this? If God is a God of love, then why does He allow the things to happen that you're going to see tonight? Where is He and why does He seem to be silent?"

As they drove the streets of inner-city Los Angeles, each one was affected by the scenes that they saw: the homeless women and children, drug deals, prostitutes (female *and* male) and fire barrels lit to provide some kind of warmth. As the van turned a corner, there in the dim streetlight a prostitute was making a score and getting into a Jeep Cherokee—off to some unknown destination. During all of this time the questions kept ringing in their ears: "Where is God in all this? Why does He seem to be silent?"

As the van arrived back at the hotel, the group shuffled into a small room off of the lobby, all the while pondering the questions. The room was uncomfortably quiet as they struggled with their emotions, trying to find some answer to the questions that were posed to them. One by one, students offered their opinions and thoughts; then it came back to the host. "Where was God tonight? Was He silent? I'll tell you where God was tonight: He was riding in a blue Dodge van. The question is not where is God in all this and does He care—the question is where are God's people who are called by His name, and do they really care enough to get involved in touching the world with His love?"

1. What did the host mean when he said "God was riding in a blue Dodge van"?

....

....

....

2. If you had been in that van, how would you have answered the question?

....

....

....

3. Do you see any situations around you where God seems to be silent?

....

....

....

 © 1996 by Gospel Light. Permission to photocopy granted.

BEING AN AGENT
OF CHANGE—
MAKING A
KINGDOM IMPACT

4. Read 2 Corinthians 5:18-20 as a group. How do these verses relate to the story?

....
....
....

What does it mean to be His ambassadors?

....
....
....

© 1996 by Gospel Light. Permission to photocopy granted.

BEING AN AGENT
OF CHANGE—
MAKING A
KINGDOM IMPACT

MAKING A KINGDOM IMPACT

The call of Christ is a call to be an agent of change. God's desire is that we reach out to those around us and make a kingdom impact one life at a time.

Read Matthew 25:31-46.

1. List all the similarities and differences between the sheep and the goats.

Similarities   Differences

....

....

....

2. How are we like the sheep in the story?

....

....

....

How are we like the goats in the story?

....

....

....

Being Sensitive to the Needs of Others

1. What is the difference between the attitude of the sheep in verse 37 and the goats in verse 44?

....

....

....

2. What keeps us from being sensitive to the needs of those around us?

....

....

....

Seeing the Face of Jesus on Those in Need

1. Who were the sheep really serving in verse 40?

....

....

....

 © 1996 by Gospel Light. Permission to photocopy granted.

2. What do you think about the statement "When you're serving those around you, you are really serving Jesus Christ"?

_____

_____

_____

3. Why do you think the goats never saw the face of Jesus in the needy ones around them?

_____

_____

_____

Serving with What You Have and Who You Are

1. What are some of the ways the sheep ministered to those around them?

_____

_____

_____

2. Why do you think the sheep were so surprised by the King's comment in verses 34-37?

_____

_____

_____

3. What do you think Jesus is calling us to do in verse 40?

_____

_____

_____

So many times we think that God is looking for the talented when in reality He is looking for the willing and available. God is looking for people who want to serve in the small things, in the "whatevers." Making a difference takes ordinary people doing ordinary things through the power of an extraordinary God.

So What?

1. What keeps you from being sensitive to the needs of those around you?

_____

_____

_____

What specific things can you do to be more sensitive to those in need?

....

....

....

2. Who in your life has the "face of Jesus"? What is God calling you to do in this person's life?

....

....

....

3. The sheep served God with what they had and who they were. What are some simple ways that you can serve God with who you are and the gifts He has given you?

....

....

....

4. What are three action steps that you will take to make a kingdom difference?

....

....

....

Action Step One:

....

....

....

Action Step Two:

....

....

....

Action Step Three:

....

....

....

 © 1996 by Gospel Light. Permission to photocopy granted.

BEING AN AGENT
OF CHANGE—
MAKING A
KINGDOM IMPACT

THE HEART
OF THE
NEW
TESTAMENT

THINGS TO THINK ABOUT

1. What are some things that you can do to make a difference in...

....

....

....

Your Church?

....

....

Your Home?

....

....

Your School?

....

....

Your Community?

....

....

2. Read Philippians 4:13. If you could make a difference for God in any way, what would you want to do?

....

....

What's keeping you from making that difference?

....

....

3. What do you think about the statement "Making a difference takes ordinary people doing ordinary things through the power of an extraordinary God"?

....

....

....

© 1996 by Gospel Light. Permission to photocopy granted.

PARENT PAGE

BE AN AGENT OF CHANGE

Being a Christian means being a part of God's plan to touch the world with His love. In Matthew 25:31-46, we hear the clear voice of God calling us to reach out to others with His love. It's more than words—it takes action!!!

What do the following passages say about making a difference for the kingdom?

....
....
....

Matthew 25:40

....
....
....

2 Corinthians 5:18-20

....
....
....

1 Thessalonians 2:8

....
....
....

1 John 3:16-18

....
....
....

Listed below are some ideas for you to be able to make a difference in your world as a family. Look through the list, brainstorm some other possible ideas, and pick one or two to get involved in as a family.

Volunteer in an area of ministry within your church.

Support a child through Compassion International:

Compassion International
P.O. Box 7000
Colorado Springs, CO 80933
1-800-336-7676

 © 1996 by Gospel Light. Permission to photocopy granted.

BEING AN AGENT
OF CHANGE—
MAKING A
KINGDOM IMPACT

Volunteer to work at a rescue mission.

As a family, volunteer at a convalescent home.

Volunteer to work with a local ministry to the homeless in your area.

Support a missionary financially and/or prayerfully.

Teach a Sunday School class as a family.

Have your pastor over for a thank-you dinner or write a note of encouragement.

Go and visit a shut-in from your church.

Open your home to a home Bible study.

Volunteer to greet visitors to your church on Sunday mornings.

Invite a new family in your church over for dinner.

Go on a short-term mission trip as a family for a weekend or a week.

Start a care ministry at your church.

Start a parent prayer support team for the youth ministry of your church.

_____ .

Session 8: "Being an Agent of Change—
Making a Kingdom Impact"

Date _____

© 1996 by Gospel Light. Permission to photocopy granted.

THE MESSAGE OF THE NEW TESTAMENT

LEADER'S PEP TALK

In the left-hand drawer of my desk I have what I call "My Encouragement File." Within this file is every note of encouragement I have ever received over the past seven years of ministry at my church. There are letters from students, parents, our senior pastor, volunteers and just about anybody who took the time to sit down and write a note. The reason I've kept all these notes? I need them!

When you're in the trenches of youth ministry, you need all the encouragement you can get. Too often it seems too little. People rarely stop you just to say thanks, but when they do, it's something to savor. If you're like me, there are days when I need to go into my office, lock the door, pull out the encouragement file and be reminded of why I do what I do and what I'm called to do. With all of the challenges that bombard us in the trenches, there are times we need to be refreshed and refocused on the task we've been called to do.

That's what the New Testament is all about. It is not only a love letter from the Father to His children, but it's also a letter of encouragement, refreshment and refocus. It's a letter to remind us that Christianity is not about what we do but about daring to be intimate with the Savior. It's a letter to remind us that God is still alive and active in our world today changing lives, hearts and circumstances. It's a letter about what's important in life: loving God with all our hearts and showing that same love to others. It's a letter sent to help us refocus our hearts and to remind us to be ready at any moment for the return of Christ.

When the storms of life seem to rage out of control, God's Word is one thing we can anchor our souls to. It's a guide to help us reset our compass. As we guide our students through the sections of the New Testament, our goal is to help them anchor their lives to the Author of these pages. So that when the storms come into their lives making it so easy to lose heart, they can open the pages of His letter and be refreshed and refocused.

> "How can a young man keep his way pure? By living according to your word. I seek you with all my heart; do not let me stray from your commands. I have hidden your word in my heart that I might not sin against you." Psalm 119:9-11

THE GOSPELS:
A RELATIONSHIP INSTEAD OF A RELIGION

KEY VERSE

"'Blessed are those who hunger and thirst for righteousness, for they will be filled.'" Matthew 5:6

BIBLICAL BASIS

Matthew 5:1-10; 20:25-28; 25:40;
Mark 1:35;
Luke 5:16; 10:38-42;
John 1:1,2,14; 4:21-24; 14:31;
Acts 2:42; 17:11;
Ephesians 5:19,20;
Philippians 3:10;
Hebrews 4:12;
1 John 3:16-18

THE BIG IDEA

The message of the Gospels is that God desires each and every person to have a vital, intimate relationship with Him. Christianity is daring to be radically intimate with the Savior.

AIMS OF THIS SESSION

During this session, you will guide students to:

- Examine the difference between a religion and a relationship with Jesus Christ;
- Discover what intimacy with the Savior means;
- Implement a plan to become more intimate with Jesus Christ.

WARM UP

THE LONGEST DISTANCE IN THE WORLD—

A story and discussion about knowing God with our hearts as well as our heads.

TEAM EFFORT— JUNIOR HIGH/ MIDDLE SCHOOL

LET ME ASK YOU A QUESTION—

Students discuss their relationships with God.

TEAM EFFORT— HIGH SCHOOL

PORTRAITS OF INTIMACY—

An activity to consider the concept of intimacy with God.

IN THE WORD

DARING TO BE INTIMATE—

A Bible study on how to have a real and intimate relationship with God.

THINGS TO THINK ABOUT (OPTIONAL)

Questions to get students thinking and talking about the levels of intimacy in their own relationships with God.

PARENT PAGE

A tool to get the session into the home and allow parents and young people to discuss how to become more intimate with God as a family.

**THE GOSPELS:
A RELATIONSHIP
INSTEAD OF
A RELIGION**

LEADER'S DEVOTIONAL

"In the beginning was the Word, and the Word was with God, and the Word was God. He was with God in the beginning. The Word became flesh and made his dwelling among us" (John 1:1,2,14).

Our home was a dive, but it was a place to live. The construction was a make-shift shack literally built around an outdoor barbecue. There was no heater. We used to turn on the oven and leave the oven door open, then sit on the door to find a touch of warmth. One ingenious roommate would take his electric blanket when he got out of bed in the morning and drag it with him around the house, plugging it in to various outlets as he worked his way around our two-bedroom box.

If you want to get to know someone very well, move in with him into a small space with some places too low to stand up straight, share limited amenities, no heat and stay put for months. When the three of us made our dwelling with each other, it forced relationships out of the cold superficial levels.

The Gospels of Jesus Christ did not simply record religious sayings and Scriptures. The Gospels unveiled the presence of God when He moved in with humanity. He entered the world in an unheated stable with a wooden feed box for a bed and animals for roommates. There was no glamour to be found in the circumstances of His birth, life or death.

Jesus came in humble, human form to bring a broken world into right relationship with a loving God. He was in a relationship as the Word and God before time. Out of this very unity of God came the impetus to put aside the divine attributes, take on the humble markings of humanity and dwell right here with us. The religious principles are present in the Gospels, but the transforming power lies in the relationship. In His final hours before His death, Jesus stated, "The world must learn that I love the Father" (John 14:31). If Jesus meant to start a religion, He chose the wrong mode of living to make His impact. Instead He turned our attention to the love between His Father and Himself. He cared more about our hearts than His home. That's good news! (Written by Doug Webster)

> **"Many people begin coming to God once they stop being religious, because there is only one master of the heart—Jesus Christ, not religion."**
> **—Oswald Chambers**

THE GOSPELS: A RELATIONSHIP INSTEAD OF A RELIGION

 ## KEY VERSE

"Blessed are those who hunger and thirst for righteousness, for they will be filled."
Matthew 5:6

BIBLICAL BASIS

Matthew 5:1-10; 20:25-28; 25:40; Luke 5:16; 10:38-42; Mark 1:35; John 1:1,2,14; 4:21-24; 14:31; Acts 2:42; 17:11; Ephesians 5:19,20; Philippians 3:10; Hebrews 4:12; 1 John 3:16-18

THE BIG IDEA

The message of the Gospels is that God desires each and every person to have a vital, intimate relationship with Him. Christianity is daring to be radically intimate with the Savior.

WARM UP (5-10 Minutes)

THE LONGEST DISTANCE IN THE WORLD

• Give each student a copy of "The Longest Distance in the World" on page 127 and have them read it. Then discuss the question at the end of the story.

• Option: Read the following story to the whole group and discuss the question.
In the Valley of the Kings stands a monument for all time—the tomb of King Tut. The excavation crew had spent years determining where the tomb was located. Finally the day had come for them to start the dig to recover one of the most prized discoveries in all the known world—the tomb of King Tut. As the dig progressed, the realization began to set in that they were in the wrong place, the tomb must be located somewhere else in the valley.

----- Fold -----

2. What does it mean that we are blessed when we recognize that we are at the end of our rope?

3. God also wants us to be broken with the things that break His heart. What do you think that means?

4. What are some of the things that break the heart of God?

RADICAL HUNGER FOR GOD (v. 6)
God calls us to have a hunger and thirst for Him.
1. What does it mean to hunger and thirst after God?

2. What are some of the things that people choose to hunger and thirst after?

3. If we choose to hunger and thirst after God, what does God promise to do?

RADICAL HEART FOR GOD (vv. 7,8)
God calls us to have an open and pure heart for Him.
1. What does it mean to have an open and pure heart towards God?

2. Why do you think God asks us to get our inside world right?

3. According to verse 8, what will be the result of getting our inside world right with Him?

SO WHAT?
1. "Christianity is daring to be intimate with the Savior." What does that mean to you?

2. How are you doing at having an intimate relationship with God? How would you rate it on a scale of 1 to 10 (1 = needs a major overhaul and 10 = cruising with Jesus)? I rate myself a ____.

3. Circle one of the following three areas in which you feel you need to become more intimate with God:
   Radical Brokenness   Radical Hunger for God   Radical Heart for God

4. What are three things that you need to do this week to cultivate that area?

THINGS TO THINK ABOUT (OPTIONAL)

• Use the questions on page 132 after or as a part of "In the Word."
1. What keeps some people from being intimate with God?
   What keeps you from being more intimate with God?
2. What are some of the benefits of having a real and intimate relationship with God as opposed to having a religion?
3. How does Philippians 3:10 relate to being intimate with God?

PARENT PAGE

• Distribute page to parents.

For the next 10 years, the excavation crew dug around the entire Valley of the Kings in search of the elusive tomb. One day the leadership team sat down to refigure their calculations. Once again, they came to the conclusion that the tomb *must* be where they had begun digging almost 10 years before.

As they reached the initial site where the quest began, Days went by. Weeks went by. Finally, a breakthrough was found. One day, as they concentrated their efforts on one particular place, they unearthed the entrance to the tomb of King Tut. Incredible celebration erupted throughout the entire team—all except for the team leader. As he walked to a nearby tent, he began to cry. His assistant ran after him.

"Why are you crying? We have just found perhaps the greatest treasure known to mankind!"

"All these years we have been searching. Yet in the end, we have wasted 10 years of our lives for a matter of a few yards."

The longest distance to travel in the world is 12 inches—the distance from your head to your heart. Too often we know about God with our head, but do we know Him with our hearts? What God desires is that we seek after Him with all our hearts, not just with our minds. God's desire is that each and every person has a vibrant love relationship with Him. Christianity is not a religion; it's a relationship. It's daring to be intimate with the Savior.

What's the difference between practicing a religion and having a relationship with God?

TEAM EFFORT—JUNIOR HIGH/MIDDLE SCHOOL (15-20 MINUTES)

LET ME ASK YOU A QUESTION

• Divide students into groups of three or four.

• Give each group a copy of "Let Me Ask You a Question" on page 128, or display a copy on an overhead projector. Have students complete the statements orally.

• Bring the groups back together and discuss their answers focusing on questions 1, 4 and 5.

1. The time I felt closest to God was...
2. When I became a Christian....
3. If I could see God face-to-face, I'd ask Him....
4. I think having a relationship with God means....
5. When I think of being real or intimate with God, I think of....

• Discuss the following questions with the whole group:

What are some of the things you do to maintain and grow a relationship with another person?

What are some things we need to do to maintain and grow a relationship with God?

TEAM EFFORT—HIGH SCHOOL (15-20 MINUTES)

PORTRAITS OF INTIMACY

• Divide the group into groups of three or four.

• Give each group three or four felt-tip pens and two pieces of poster board.

• Have students draw a picture of what intimacy means to the members of their group on one of the pieces of poster board. On the other piece of poster board, have them draw a picture of what it means to be intimate with God.

• Spend a few minutes having each group describe their portraits of intimacy.

IN THE WORD (25-30 MINUTES)

DARING TO BE INTIMATE

• Divide students into groups of three or four.

• Give each student a copy of "Daring to Be Intimate" on pages 129-131 and a pen or pencil, or display a copy on an overhead projector.

• Have students complete the Bible study.

The message of the Gospels is that God desires each and every person to have a vital, intimate relationship with Him and not just a stale religion. Christianity in its truest sense is daring to be intimate with God.

Read the following section of Scripture:

When Jesus saw his ministry drawing huge crowds, he climbed a hillside. Those who were apprenticed to him, the committed, climbed with him. Arriving at a quiet place, he sat down and taught his climbing companions. This is what he said:

"You're blessed when you're at the end of your rope. With less of you there is more of God and his rule.

"You're blessed when you feel you've lost what is most dear to you. Only then can you be embraced by the One most dear to you.

"You're blessed when you're content with just who you are—no more, no less. That's the moment you find yourselves the proud owners of everything that can't be bought.

"You're blessed when you've worked up a good appetite for God. He's food and drink in the best meal you'll ever eat.

"You're blessed when you care. At the moment of being 'care-full,' you find yourselves cared for.

"You're blessed when you get your inside world—your mind and heart—put right. Then you can see God in the outside world.

"You're blessed when you can show people how to cooperate instead of compete or fight. That's when you discover who you really are, and your place in God's family.

"You're blessed when your commitment to God provokes persecution. The persecution drives you even deeper into God's Kingdom" (Matthew 5:1-10, *The Message*).

Being intimate with the Savior is marked by three things:

RADICAL BROKENNESS (vv. 3-5)

God calls us to be broken over our sin and for others.

1. Why is it tough to admit that we are spiritually at the end of our rope and in need of a Savior?

WARM UP

THE LONGEST DISTANCE IN THE WORLD

In the Valley of the Kings stands a monument for all time—the tomb of King Tut. The excavation crew had spent years determining where the tomb was located. Finally the day had come for them to start the dig to recover one of the most prized discoveries in all the known world—the tomb of King Tut. As the dig progressed, the realization began to set in that they were in the wrong place, the tomb must be located somewhere else in the valley.

For the next 10 years, the excavation crew dug around the entire Valley of the Kings in search of the elusive tomb. One day the leadership team sat down to refigure their calculations. Once again, they came to the conclusion that the tomb *must* be where they had begun digging almost 10 years before.

As they reached the initial site where the quest began, the decision was made to dig around the site in hopes of possibly finding the entrance to the tomb. Days went by. Weeks went by. Finally, a breakthrough was made. One day, as they concentrated their efforts on one particular place, they unearthed the entrance to the tomb of King Tut. Incredible celebration erupted throughout the entire team—all except for the team leader. As he walked to a nearby tent, he began to cry. His assistant ran after him.

"Why are you crying? We have just found perhaps the greatest treasure known to mankind!"

"All these years we have been searching. Yet in the end, we have wasted 10 years of our lives for a matter of a few yards."

The longest distance to travel in the world is 12 inches—the distance from your head to your heart. Too often we know about God with our head, but do we know Him with our hearts? What God desires is that we seek after Him with all our hearts, not just with our minds. God's desire is that each and every person has a vibrant love relationship with Him. Christianity is not a religion; it's a relationship. It's daring to be intimate with the Savior.

What's the difference between practicing a religion and having a relationship with God?

 © 1996 by Gospel Light. Permission to photocopy granted.

TEAM EFFORT

LET ME ASK YOU A QUESTION

1. The time I felt closest to God was...

....

....

....

2. When I became a Christian...

....

....

....

3. If I could see God face-to-face, I'd ask Him...

....

....

....

4. I think having a relationship with God means...

....

....

....

5. When I think of being real or intimate with God, I think of...

....

....

....

© 1996 by Gospel Light. Permission to photocopy granted.

THE GOSPELS:
A RELATIONSHIP
INSTEAD OF
A RELIGION

DARING TO BE INTIMATE

The message of the Gospels is that God desires each and every person to have a vital, intimate relationship with Him, not just a stale religion. Christianity in its truest sense is daring to be intimate with God.

Read the following section of Scripture:

When Jesus saw his ministry drawing huge crowds, he climbed a hillside. Those who were apprenticed to him, the committed, climbed with him. Arriving at a quiet place, he sat down and taught his climbing companions. This is what he said:

"You're blessed when you're at the end of your rope. With less of you there is more of God and his rule.

"You're blessed when you feel you've lost what is most dear to you. Only then can you be embraced by the One most dear to you.

"You're blessed when you're content with just who you are— no more, no less. That's the moment you find yourselves the proud owners of everything that can't be bought.

"You're blessed when you've worked up a good appetite for God. He's food and drink in the best meal you'll ever eat.

"You're blessed when you care. At the moment of being 'care-full,' you find yourselves cared for.

"You're blessed when you get your inside world—your mind and heart—put right. Then you can see God in the outside world.

"You're blessed when you can show people how to cooperate instead of compete or fight. That's when you discover who you really are, and your place in God's family.

"You're blessed when your commitment to God provokes persecution. The persecution drives you even deeper into God's Kingdom" (Matthew 5:1-10, *The Message*).

 © 1996 by Gospel Light. Permission to photocopy granted.

THE GOSPELS:
A RELATIONSHIP
INSTEAD OF
A RELIGION

Being intimate with the Savior is marked by three things:

Radical Brokenness (vv. 3-5)

God calls us to be broken over our sin and for others.

1. Why is it tough to admit that we are spiritually at the end of our rope and in need of a Savior?

....
....
....

2. What does it mean that we are blessed when we recognize that we are at the end of our rope?

....
....
....

3. God also wants us to be broken with the things that break His heart. What do you think that means?

....
....
....

4. What are some of the things that break the heart of God?

....
....
....

Radical Hunger for God (v. 6)

God calls us to have a hunger and thirst for Him.

1. What does it mean to hunger and thirst after God?

....
....
....

2. What are some of the things that people choose to hunger and thirst after?

....
....
....

© 1996 by Gospel Light. Permission to photocopy granted.

3. If we choose to hunger and thirst after God, what does God promise to do?

....

....

Radical Heart for God (vv. 7,8)
God calls us to have an open and pure heart for Him.

1. What does it mean to have an open and pure heart towards God?

....

....

....

2. Why do you think God asks us to get our inside world put right?

....

....

....

3. According to verse 8, what will be the result of getting our inside world right with Him?

....

....

....

So What?

1. "Christianity is daring to be intimate with the Savior." What does that mean to you?

....

....

....

2. How are you doing at having an intimate relationship with God? How would you rate it on a scale of 1 to 10
   (1 = needs a major overhaul and 10 = cruising with Jesus)? I rate myself a _____ .

3. Circle one of the following three areas in which you feel you need to become more intimate with God:

Radical Brokenness   Radical Hunger for God   Radical Heart for God

4. What are three things that you need to do this week to cultivate that area?

....

....

....

 © 1996 by Gospel Light. Permission to photocopy granted.

THE GOSPELS:
A RELATIONSHIP
INSTEAD OF
A RELIGION

THINGS TO THINK ABOUT

1. What keeps some people from being intimate with God?

    ....
    ....
    ....

    What keeps you from being more intimate with God?

    ....
    ....
    ....

2. What are some of the benefits of having a real and intimate relationship with God as opposed to having a religion?

    ....
    ....
    ....

3. How does Philippians 3:10 relate to being intimate with God?

    ....
    ....
    ....

**THE GOSPELS:
A RELATIONSHIP
INSTEAD OF
A RELIGION**

PARENT PAGE

PROFILES IN INTIMACY

Christianity is daring to be intimate with the Savior. Christianity is about having a living, vital and growing relationship with God. It's not about what church you go to or about what religion you practice. Christianity is about a relationship with a living God who knows you and desires you to know Him. In the Scriptures below are four areas in which we grow in our intimacy with God. As a family, read the Scriptures and identify the avenues by which we can grow more intimate with the Savior.

Luke 10:38-42; Acts 17:11; Hebrews 4:12 _____

Mark 1:35; Luke 5:16; Acts 2:42 _____

John 4:21-24; Ephesians 5:19,20 _____

Matthew 20:25-28; 25:40; 1 John 3:16-18 _____

As a family, come up with as many ideas as you can about what you can do as a family to grow more intimate with God through the following areas. Here are a few ideas to get you started:

God's Word

1. Start having a regular family devotion or Bible study time.
2. Memorize Scripture together as a family.
3. _____
4. _____
5. _____

Prayer

1. Pray together daily as a family.
2. Create a prayer calendar of people and issues to pray over.
3. _____
4. _____
5. _____

Worship

1. Attend worship services regularly at your church as a family.
2. Have a worship service in your home complete with singing, Scripture reading, a devotional, etc.
3. _____
4. _____
5. _____

Now circle one of the options in each category and over the next few weeks make those elements a regular part of your family's life.

Service

1. Serve in an area of ministry in your church as a family.
2. Serve in a homeless shelter as a family.
3. _____
4. _____
5. _____

Session 9: "The Gospels: A Relationship Instead of a Religion" Date _____

 © 1996 by Gospel Light. Permission to photocopy granted.

ACTS:
THE LIFE-CHANGING POWER OF GOD

K EY VERSE

"But you will receive power when the Holy Spirit comes on you; and you will be my witnesses in Jerusalem, and in all Judea and Samaria, and to the ends of the earth." Acts 1:8

B IBLICAL BASIS

Luke 18:35-43;
Acts 1:3,8; 3:1-10, 4:13; 12:5-11; 16:25-34;
Philippians 4:6,7

T HE BIG IDEA

The message of Acts is that God is active and about the business of changing lives, circumstances and hearts.

A IMS OF THIS SESSION

During this session, you will guide students to:
• Examine God's power as displayed in the book of Acts;
• Discover how the power of God can affect everyday life;
• Implement a new awareness of the power of God in everyday life.

W ARM UP

INDOOR SCAVENGER HUNT—
A game to break the ice.

T EAM EFFORT— JUNIOR HIGH/ MIDDLE SCHOOL

THE POWER OF GOD AND OUR WORLD: FRONT PAGE NEWS—
Students consider whether or not God is at work in the world today.

T EAM EFFORT— HIGH SCHOOL

PORTRAYALS OF POWER—
Students role-play three scenes from the book of Acts.

I N THE WORD

TAPPING INTO OUR POWER SOURCE
A Bible study on God's power to change lives and circumstances.

T HINGS TO THINK ABOUT (OPTIONAL)

Questions to get students thinking and talking about how the power of God is manifested in their lives and the lives of others.

P ARENT PAGE

A tool to get the session into the home and allow parents and young people to discuss how to tap into the power of God that is available to all believers.

ACTS:
THE LIFE-
CHANGING
POWER OF GOD

LEADER'S DEVOTIONAL

"After [Jesus'] suffering, he showed himself to these men and gave many convincing proofs that he was alive" (Acts 1:3).

"The proof is in the pudding" the kitchen axiom goes. It all depends on how it tastes when the stove has cooled and the pudding is served. The Acts of the apostles is the bridge between the good news revealed in the historic human life of Jesus Christ and the Church guiding and building epistles. The book of Acts is Christianity's "proof in the pudding."

Acts offers the Church four vital aspects of the faith: the proof of the historic launching of the Church; the apologetics of the faith to both Jews and Gentiles; the guidebook by which to live as a follower of Christ; and the triumph of Christianity as a work of God's power more than a man-made religion.

In the fourth chapter of the book of Acts, Peter and John were imprisoned for their faith. They created quite an uproar through their testimony of the power and presence of the risen Jesus Christ. Thousands were added as followers of Christ. They found themselves in the presence of the religious leaders of their day. The high priest and his family inquired of Peter and John's source of power. Peter gave direct attention to Jesus Christ of Nazareth, the Man crucified and now resurrected, as the source of salvation and healing for humanity. Scripture states "When they saw the courage of Peter and John and realized that they were unschooled, ordinary men, they were astonished and they took note that these men had been with Jesus" (Acts 4:13).

Peter, the same man who sank like a rock under the pressure of fear, stood strong as a rock in the face of pending incarceration and death. Why? It wasn't his academic acumen, nor his extraordinary abilities—the life-changing power of God filled Peter. The power of the new Church stemmed from some rather ordinary people who had been with Jesus.

Do you find power in your life these days? Do you see the life-transforming power of Christ adding people to your fellowship and healing the crippled around you? The power of God is fleshed out in the acts of His people who spend time in the presence of Christ before doing His work.

Before you launch into more ministry or the next curriculum of teaching, take a few extra moments to be with Jesus. You will be renewed by His presence and reminded of the life-changing power of the bearer of the Church's name, Jesus Christ. (Written by Doug Webster)

"Be assured, if you walk with Him and look to Him and expect help from Him, He will never fail you."
—George Mueller

ACTS:
THE LIFE-CHANGING POWER OF GOD

Key Verse

"But you will receive power when the Holy Spirit comes on you; and you will be my witnesses in Jerusalem, and in all Judea and Samaria, and to the ends of the earth." Acts 1:8

Biblical Basis

Luke 18:35-43; Acts 1:3,8; 3:1-10; 4:13; 12:5-11; 16:25-34; Philippians 4:6,7

The Big Idea

The message of Acts is that God is active and about the business of changing lives, circumstances and hearts.

Warm Up (5-10 Minutes)

Indoor Scavenger Hunt

- Divide the students into two approximately equal groups (don't worry about it being exact).
- Tell them that you will be asking them to find ordinary (and not so ordinary) items one at a time.
- The first group to produce the item wins that round. You can provide prizes or freebies for the winning team or for any individual round. Here's a *sample* list of items to ask for:

    A picture of your mother
    A picture of a pet
    A bad driver's license picture
    A paper clip
    A safety pin

----- Fold -----

2. What are the characteristics of a hard heart?

3. What are the characteristics of a changed heart?

4. Why does God sometimes need to use the miraculous to break our hearts?

5. How did the jailer respond to what happened in the jail that night?

So What?

1. Where do you see God working in your life today?

2. Where do you need God's power to change your...

Life?

Circumstances?

Heart?

Things to Think About (optional)

- Use the questions on page 142 after or as a part of "In the Word."

1. How can you reach out to those who are on the outside of God's family with the power and love of God?
2. Who do you know around you that needs a changed heart? What can you do in that person's life?
3. Why is it difficult sometimes to see the power of God working in our lives? In others' lives?
4. Why does God sometimes choose not to change our circumstances?

Parent Page

- Distribute page to parents.

Four shoe strings tied end-to-end (without the shoes!)
The largest shoe from your group
The smallest shoe from your group
Someone who failed their driver's test the first time
The person with the earliest "first crush"
The person who works at a fast food restaurant
The person with the most creative dating experience
Someone who has traveled the farthest away from home
Someone who has met a celebrity
The strangest item you can produce

TEAM EFFORT—JUNIOR HIGH/MIDDLE SCHOOL (15-20 Minutes)

THE POWER OF GOD AND OUR WORLD: FRONT PAGE NEWS

• Before coming to the group, either pick up a copy of today's newspaper or videotape the first 5-10 minutes of a news broadcast. The idea is to bring students face-to-face with God's power in light of current events.

• Show a video clip from the newscast (the first three to five minutes usually works well), read an article from the day's front page, or divide students into smaller groups and give them a copy of the front page to look at.

• Discuss the following questions:

1. Where is God's power today?

   How is He at work in today's current events?

2. Does He seem to be silent? Why or Why not?

3. How does our world view the power of God?

4. Was there a time when you experienced the power of God in your own life?

5. How do you think God works in our world today?

TEAM EFFORT—HIGH SCHOOL (15-20 Minutes)

PORTRAYALS OF POWER

• Divide students into three equal groups.

• Assign each group one of the following passages:

   Scene One: Acts 3:1-10

   Scene Two: Acts 12:5-11

   Scene Three: Acts 16:25-34

• Tell them to come up with their own dramatic representation of their scene. Encourage your students to have fun, modernize and add their own creativity or humor to their presentation.

• After each group gets an opportunity to share their drama, discuss the following questions.

1. How was the power of God displayed in each of the scenes?

2. What did the three scenes have in common? (prayer, praising God, thanking Him in response, giving Him the credit, someone was changed, etc.)

3. What did you learn about the power of God from these three scenes?

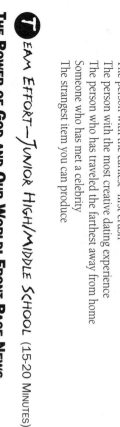

IN THE WORD (25-30 Minutes)

TAPPING INTO OUR POWER SOURCE

• Divide students into groups of three or four.

• Give each student a copy of "Tapping into Our Power Source" on pages 139-141 and a pen or pencil, or display a copy on an overhead projector.

• Have students complete the Bible study.

God is in the business of building His kingdom and changing lives. God is powerful and active in our world today, just as He was in the book of Acts. Yet more often than not, we miss the true power of God in our world today. God is active and wants to change lives, circumstances and hearts!

SCENE ONE—ACTS 3:1-10: THE POWER OF GOD AND A CHANGED LIFE

In Acts 3:1-10, we see a man crippled since birth, lacking hope of ever being healed, about to come face-to-face with the power of God. Just like him, there are people who go through life crippled in body and spirit, desperately begging for some direction and healing. Maybe that's you or someone you know. Everyone is in need of the life-changing power of God.

1. How do you think the crippled man felt listening to the words of Peter?

2. How did the crippled man respond to the miraculous healing?

3. The man was on the outside. When was a time that you felt on the outside?

4. Peter gave what he had to the man. How can we change other's lives by giving what we have?

....

SCENE TWO—ACTS 12:5-11: THE POWER OF GOD AND CHANGED CIRCUMSTANCES

Not only is God in the business of changing lives, He's also in the business of changing situations and circumstances and freeing people. Sometimes our circumstances seem like chains that bind us. In Acts 12:5-11, God rescued Peter out of what seemed a pretty hopeless situation because God's people were praying.

1. What would be your response to being unjustly imprisoned?

2. In the prison, the soldiers had Peter bound in chains. What are some issues or situations that bind teenagers today making it seem impossible to escape?

3. Why is it tough to look past our circumstances to the power of God?

4. Read Philippians 4:6,7. How can prayer free us from circumstances and things that may weigh us down?

....

SCENE THREE—ACTS 16:25-34: THE POWER OF GOD AND A CHANGED HEART

God also has the power to break into a hard heart to change it. As Paul and Silas were in prison, God not only shook the walls of the prison but also the walls of the jailer's hardened heart.

1. What are some of the things that cause our hearts to be hardened today?

....

 IN THE WORD

TAPPING INTO OUR POWER SOURCE

God is in the business of building the Kingdom and changing lives. God is powerful and active in our world today, just as He was in the book of Acts. Yet more often than not, we miss the true power of God in our world today. God is active and wants to change lives, circumstances and hearts!

Scene One—Acts 3:1-10: The Power of God and a Changed Life

In Acts 3:1-10, we see a man crippled since birth, lacking hope for ever being healed, about to come face-to-face with the power of God. Just like him, there are people who go through life crippled in body and spirit, desperately begging for some direction and healing. Maybe that's you or someone you know. Everyone is in need of the life-changing power of God.

1. How do you think the crippled man felt listening to the words of Peter?

_____

_____

_____

2. How did the crippled man respond to the miraculous healing?

_____

_____

_____

3. The man was on the outside. When was a time that you felt on the outside?

_____

_____

_____

4. Peter gave what he had to the man. How can we change others' lives by giving what we have?

_____

_____

_____

Scene Two—Acts 12:5-11: The Power of God and Changed Circumstances

Not only is God in the business of changing lives, He's also in the business of changing situations and circumstances and freeing people. Sometimes our circumstances seem like chains that bind us. In Acts 12:5-11, because God's people were praying, God rescued Peter out of what seemed a pretty hopeless situation.

 © 1996 by Gospel Light. Permission to photocopy granted.

ACTS:
THE LIFE-
CHANGING
POWER OF GOD

1. What would be your response to being unjustly imprisoned?

....

....

2. In the prison, the soldiers had Peter bound in chains. What are some issues or situations that bind teenagers today, making it seem impossible to escape?

....

....

3. Why is it tough to look past our circumstances to the power of God?

....

....

4. Read Philippians 4:6,7. How can prayer free us from circumstances and things that may weigh us down?

....

....

Scene Three—Acts 16:25-34: The Power of God and a Changed Heart

God also has the power to break through a hard heart to change it. As Paul and Silas were in prison, God not only shook the walls of the prison but also the walls of the jailer's hardened heart.

1. What are some of the things that cause our hearts to be hardened today?

....

....

2. What are the characteristics of a hard heart?

....

....

....

© 1996 by Gospel Light. Permission to photocopy granted.

3. What are the characteristics of a changed heart?

_____

_____

_____

4. Why does God sometimes need to use the miraculous to break our hearts?

_____

_____

_____

5. How did the jailer respond to what happened in the jail that night?

_____

_____

_____

So What?

1. Where do you see God working in your life today?

_____

_____

_____

2. Where do you need God's power to change your...

_____

_____

_____

Life?

_____

_____

Circumstances?

_____

_____

_____

Heart?

_____

_____

_____

_____

 © 1996 by Gospel Light. Permission to photocopy granted.

ACTS:
THE LIFE-
CHANGING
POWER OF GOD

Things to Think About

1. How can you reach out to those who are on the outside of God's family with the power and love of God?

....

....

....

2. Who do you know around you that needs a changed heart? What can you do in that person's life?

....

....

....

3. Why is it difficult sometimes to see the power of God working in our lives?

....

....

....

    In others' lives?

....

....

....

4. Why does God sometimes choose not to change our circumstances?

....

....

....

PARENT PAGE

"WHAT DO YOU WANT ME TO DO FOR YOU?"

God is alive and at work in our world today. All we need to do is look around and we'll see His handiwork and His power. We can see it in the mountains, hear it in a baby's cry and see it in a changed life. He's at work in broken people's lives, seemingly insurmountable situations and hardened hearts. Just as in the New Testament, Jesus is active in changing lives today. How about yours?

As Jesus approached Jericho, a blind man was sitting by the roadside begging. When he heard the crowd going by, he asked what was happening. They told him, "Jesus of Nazareth is passing by."

He called out, "Jesus, Son of David, have mercy on me!"

Those who led the way rebuked him and told him to be quiet, but he shouted all the more, "Son of David, have mercy on me!"

Jesus stopped and ordered the man to be brought to him. When he came near, Jesus asked him, "What do you want me to do for you?"

"Lord, I want to see," he replied.

Jesus said to him, "Receive your sight; your faith has healed you." Immediately he received his sight and followed Jesus, praising God. When all the people saw it, they also praised God (Luke 18:35-43).

1. What keeps us from calling out to God when we have a need?

....

....

....

2. When was there a time that you needed God's power to change you?

....

....

....

 © 1996 by Gospel Light. Permission to photocopy granted.

ACTS:
THE LIFE-
CHANGING
POWER OF GOD

3. How would you answer Jesus if He asked you, "What do you want me to do for you?"

....

....

What do you need God's power to change in your...

....

....

Life?

....

....

To experience change in your life you need prayer and a plan to pursue.

Circumstances?

....

....

Prayer:
Look at the areas listed and spend some time in prayer, asking God to help make a change in your life.

Heart?

....

....

Plan:
Take a moment to write out a plan for some things that must happen before that change can occur in your life.

PUTTING THE PIECES IN PLACE

1. What is the common ingredient that put the power of God in motion in Acts 12:5-11 and in Acts 16:25-34?

....

....

....

Pursue:
Take a few minutes and ask God to give you the strength to pursue your plan. Ask Him to act powerfully in your life.

2. What does Philippians 4:6,7 have to say about prayer?

....

....

....

Session 10: "Acts: The Life-Changing Power of God" Date ....

© 1996 by Gospel Light. Permission to photocopy granted.

THE LETTERS:
THE OWNER'S MANUAL

KEY VERSE

"And this is love: that we walk in obedience to his commands. As you have heard from the beginning, his command is that you walk in love."
2 John 6

BIBLICAL BASIS

Matthew 22:37-40;
Romans 11:34; 12:2; 13:8-10;
1 Corinthians 2:16; 13:1-8;
Philippians 2:1-5;
James 2:15-17;
1 Peter 1:13-16;
1 John 2:3-6; 3:16-18; 5:2,3;
2 John 6

THE BIG IDEA

The message of the letters is that the Christian life is to be lived loving God and others.

AIMS OF THIS SESSION

During this session, you will guide students to:
- Examine the themes of loving God and loving others found in the letters;
- Discover how loving God and others is lived out in life;
- Implement a decision and action steps to live a life of obedience, holiness and a commitment to serving others.

WARM UP

INVENTORY OF LOVE—
Students take an inventory of their level of love for God and for others.

TEAM EFFORT— JUNIOR HIGH/ MIDDLE SCHOOL

LETTERS—
Students compose letters of encouragement and instruction to their youth group.

TEAM EFFORT— HIGH SCHOOL

TELEMACHUS: A SNAPSHOT OF LOVE AND OBEDIENCE—
The story of a humble, obedient man who changed a city.

IN THE WORD

CHECKING OUT THE OWNER'S MANUAL—
A Bible study on how to live out your faith and relationship with God every day.

THINGS TO THINK ABOUT (OPTIONAL)

Questions to get students thinking and talking about how to love God and others.

PARENT PAGE

A tool to get the session into the home and allow parents and young people to discuss ways to express their love to God and others.

THE LETTERS:
THE OWNER'S
MANUAL

LEADER'S DEVOTIONAL

"But we have the mind of Christ" (1 Corinthians 2:16).

I am not a good instructions-manual person. I don't abandon them to the trash and strike out on my own. I'm not that bad. On the other hand, I have an undefined but very clear statute of limitations that reaches its point of disinterest after a period of time. I can't tell you when, I just know I say to myself "Oh, forget it. Just give it to me. I'll make it work." Undoubtedly, I'll end up breaking something and have to spend twice as much time and money for repairs.

How about you? Which of the three roads do you take? Are you...

1. An instructions junkie?
2. A glance-and-go-getter?
3. An abandon-and-attack animal?

If you're not sure, take a quick glance at the VCR in your home. If the clock is flashing 12:00, you're definitely not a number one. Now roll the video depicting your faith and ministry leadership. Which of the above three levels describes your study of God's Word?

The letters of the apostles serve as the guidebook or instruction manual to a growing faith in Christ. On numerous occasions, Paul speaks of believers as being "in Christ" which is every believer's position before our Holy God. What does it mean to be in Christ? It means to put your life in Jesus, and His life in you taking on not only His presence and His name, but His very mind. Can you think of a more incredible reality than obtaining the mind of Christ?

Read 2:16 in Paul's first letter to the church at Corinth. Read Paul's words to the Romans in 11:34 and 12:2. Still not convinced you can have the mind of Jesus? Check out Paul's letter to the church at Philippi in the second chapter, verses 2 and 5. The New Testament letters won't teach you how to change your flashing clock or to use a spell check program, but they are the owner's manual to your faith. Our purpose is not to become more educated owners but to learn to think, pray, believe, act and live like Christ, the owner of our Christian lives.

Next time your life hits a flashing point and you're making terrible time, drop the tools and pick up the manual. Read a letter from your Owner to you. You're bound to rebound and find the right way to program this thing called life. (Written by Doug Webster)

"Education is what you get from reading the small print in a contract. Experience is what you get from not reading it."
—Anonymous

THE LETTERS: THE OWNER'S MANUAL

ⓀEY VERSE

"And this is love: that we walk in obedience to his commands. As you have heard from the beginning, his command is that you walk in love." 2 John 6

ⒷIBLICAL BASIS

Matthew 22:37-40; Romans 11:34; 12:2; 13:8-10; 1 Corinthians 2:16; 13:1-8; Philippians 2:1-5; James 2:15-17; 1 Peter 1:13-16; 1 John 2:3-6; 3:16-18; 5:2,3; 2 John 6

ⓉHE BIG IDEA

The message of the letters is that the Christian life is to be lived loving God and others.

ⓌARM UP (5-10 MINUTES)

INVENTORY OF LOVE

• Give each student a copy of "Inventory of Love" on page 149 and a pen or pencil.
• Have them complete the following inventory to examine where they are in their love for God and others. Below each statement is a scale from 1 to 10.

One of the themes running throughout the letters of the New Testament is the theme of loving God and others. Circle where you are according to each statement (1 = needs some work and 10 = doing great in this area).

| 1 | 2 | 3 | 4 | 5 | 6 | 7 | 8 | 9 | 10 |

I spend time with God on a regular basis in His Word.

| 1 | 2 | 3 | 4 | 5 | 6 | 7 | 8 | 9 | 10 |

I regularly tell God how much I love Him.

--- Fold ---

LOVING OTHERS—GIVING YOURSELF TO OTHERS

1. In Romans 13:8-10, in what area do we have a debt to one another?

2. What can you do to "love your neighbor as yourself"?

3. In Philippians 2:4, we are called to "look out for the interests of others." What keeps us from living out this verse?

4. Read James 2:15-17 and 1 John 3:16-18. What do these passages say about loving others?

What keeps us from doing that?

5. What are some practical ways we can put our love for others into action?

SO WHAT?

1. In what areas do you need to obey God more?

What will you do to give yourself more to God?

2. In what areas of your life do you need to strive to be more holy?

What choices do you need to make?

How can this group help?

3. Who is someone right now in your life that needs your love?

What will you do to show love to that person?

ⓉHINGS TO THINK ABOUT (OPTIONAL)

• Use the questions on page 156 after or as a part of "In the Word."

1. What are some things that come between us and our love for God?
2. Why do God's commands seem burdensome?
3. In what ways has God demonstrated His love for you?
4. What are some things that keep you from putting your love into action?

ⓅARENT PAGE

• Distribute page to parents.

I seek to love God more in my life.

| 1 | 2 | 3 | 4 | 5 | 6 | 7 | 8 | 9 | 10 |

I understand what it means to love God.

| 1 | 2 | 3 | 4 | 5 | 6 | 7 | 8 | 9 | 10 |

My love for God impacts how I live my life.

| 1 | 2 | 3 | 4 | 5 | 6 | 7 | 8 | 9 | 10 |

My love for God impacts how I treat others.

| 1 | 2 | 3 | 4 | 5 | 6 | 7 | 8 | 9 | 10 |

I have a hard time loving others.

| 1 | 2 | 3 | 4 | 5 | 6 | 7 | 8 | 9 | 10 |

I seek to be others-centered in my life

| 1 | 2 | 3 | 4 | 5 | 6 | 7 | 8 | 9 | 10 |

I am actively involved in serving and loving others.

| 1 | 2 | 3 | 4 | 5 | 6 | 7 | 8 | 9 | 10 |

I regularly reach out to try and help those in need.

| 1 | 2 | 3 | 4 | 5 | 6 | 7 | 8 | 9 | 10 |

1. How would you describe what it means to love God?
2. How would you describe what it means to love others?
3. Which is more difficult for you and why?

TEAM EFFORT—JUNIOR HIGH/MIDDLE SCHOOL (15-20 MINUTES)

LETTERS

• Tell the group that today they will be taking a look at the message of the letters of the New Testament. Let them know that the major purpose in the writing of the letters was to encourage and instruct Christians on how to live the Christian life in their everyday world.
• Divide students into groups of three or four.
• Give each group paper and pens or pencils.
• Have each group write a short letter as if they were one of the letter writers of the New Testament. Have them address their letter to their youth group. In the letter, tell them to encourage and instruct the group in their relationship with Christ and others in the youth group.
• After 5 to 10 minutes or so, have a few of the groups share their letters with the entire group.

TELEMACHUS: A SNAPSHOT OF LOVE AND OBEDIENCE

• Read the story "Telemachus: A Snapshot of Love and Obedience" on pages 154-155 to the whole group.
• Or make several copies and ask for volunteers to read the story.
• Discuss the questions which follow the story.

Fold

1. How would you describe Telemachus's relationship with God?
2. How did he live out his love for God?
3. What do you think Telemachus felt when he was in the Coliseum?
4. How did he live out his love for others?
5. What is the message of this true story for you and me?

IN THE WORD (25-30 MINUTES)

CHECKING OUT THE OWNER'S MANUAL

• Divide students into groups of three or four.
• Give each student a copy of "In the Word" on pages 152-155 and a pen or pencil, or display a copy on an overhead projector.
• Have students complete the Bible study.

The letters were written to be an encouragement and an instruction manual for living the Christian life every day. They were written to be a guidebook on issues regarding our Christian life to help us live out our faith and relationship with God every day. One of the greatest themes in the letters is that of loving God and loving others.

LOVING GOD—GIVING YOURSELF TO GOD

Obedience—Read 1 John 2:3-5 and 1 John 5:2,3
1. How do these passages define what it means to love God?

2. If we love God, why won't His commandments seem burdensome?

3. Where does following God's commandments fall for you?

Burdensome									Joyful
1	2	3	4	5	6	7	8	9	10

Holiness—Read 1 Peter 1:13-16
1. What does it mean to be holy as God is holy?

2. In what areas do we need to live more holy lives?

3. How does living a life of holiness express our love for God?

4. What are we called to do in 1 John 2:6?
What does that mean?

5. What are some of the ways we can walk as Jesus did?

Warm Up

INVENTORY OF LOVE

One of the themes running throughout the New Testament is the theme of loving God and others. Circle where you are according to each statement (1 = needs some work, and 10 = doing great in this area).

I regularly tell God how much I love Him.

1   2   3   4   5   6   7   8   9   10

I spend time with God on a regular basis in His Word.

1   2   3   4   5   6   7   8   9   10

I seek to love God more in my life.

1   2   3   4   5   6   7   8   9   10

I understand what it means to love God.

1   2   3   4   5   6   7   8   9   10

My love for God impacts how I live my life.

1   2   3   4   5   6   7   8   9   10

My love for God impacts how I treat others.

1   2   3   4   5   6   7   8   9   10

I have a hard time loving others.

1   2   3   4   5   6   7   8   9   10

I seek to be others-centered in my life.

1   2   3   4   5   6   7   8   9   10

I am actively involved in serving and loving others.

1   2   3   4   5   6   7   8   9   10

I regularly reach out to try and help those in need.

1   2   3   4   5   6   7   8   9   10

1. How would you describe what it means to love God?

....

....

....

2. How would you describe what it means to love others?

....

....

....

3. Which is more difficult for you and why?

....

....

....

 © 1996 by Gospel Light. Permission to photocopy granted.

TEAM EFFORT

TELEMACHUS: A SNAPSHOT OF LOVE AND OBEDIENCE

In the fourth century there lived an Asiatic monk who spent most of his life in a remote community of prayer, raising vegetables for the cloister kitchen. When he was not tending his garden spot, he was fulfilling his vocation of study and prayer.

Then one day this monk named Telemachus felt that the Lord wanted him to go to Rome, the capital of the world. Telemachus had no idea why he should go there, and he was terrified at the thought. But as he prayed, God's directive became clear.

How bewildered the little monk must have been as he set out on the long journey on foot over the dusty roads westward, everything he owned on his back. Why was he going? He didn't know. What would he find there? He had no idea. But obediently, he went.

Telemachus arrived in Rome during the holiday festival. You may know that the Roman rulers kept the ghettos quiet in those days by providing free bread and special entertainment called circuses. At the time Telemachus arrived, the city was bustling with excitement over the recent Roman victory over the Goths. In the midst of this jubilant commotion, the monk looked for clues as to why God had brought him there, for he had no other guidance, not even a superior in a religious order to contact.

"Perhaps," he thought, "it is not sheer coincidence that I have arrived at the festival time. Perhaps God has some special role for me to play."

So Telemachus let the crowds guide him, and the stream of humanity soon led him into the Coliseum where the gladiator contests were to be staged. He could hear the cries of the animals in their cages beneath the floor of the great arena and the clamor of the contestants preparing to do battle.

The gladiators marched into the arena, saluted the emperor and shouted, "We who are about to die salute thee." Telemachus shuddered. He had never heard of the gladiator games before, but had a premonition of awful violence.

The crowd had come to cheer men who, for no reason other than amusement, would murder each other. Human lives were offered for entertainment. As the monk realized what was going to happen, he realized that he could not sit still and watch such savagery. Neither could he leave and forget. He jumped to the top of the perimeter wall and cried, "In the name of Christ, forbear!"

The fighting began, of course. No one paid the slightest heed to the puny voice. So Telemachus pattered down the stone steps and leapt onto the sandy floor of the arena. He made a comic figure—a scrawny man in a monk's habit dashing back and forth between muscular, armed athletes. One gladiator sent him sprawling with a blow from his shield, directing him back to his seat. It was a rough gesture, though almost a kind one. The crowd roared.

But Telemachus refused to stop. He rushed into the way of those trying to fight, shouting again, "In the name of Christ, forbear!" The crowd began to laugh and cheer him on, perhaps thinking him part of the entertainment.

Then his movement blocked the vision of one of the contestants and the gladiator saw the blow coming just in time. Furious now, the crowd began to cry for the interloper's blood.

"Run him through," they screamed.

© 1996 by Gospel Light. Permission to photocopy granted.

The gladiator he had blocked raised his sword and with a flash of steel struck Telemachus, slashing down across his chest and into his stomach. The little monk gasped once more, "In the name of Christ, forbear."

Then a strange thing occurred. As the two gladiators and the crowd focused on the still form on the suddenly crimson sand, the arena grew deathly quiet. In the silence, someone on the top tier got up and walked out. Another followed. All over the arena, spectators began to leave, until the huge stadium was emptied.

There were other forces at work, of course, but that innocent figure lying in a pool of blood crystallized the opposition, and that was the last gladiatorial contest in the Roman Coliseum. Never again did men kill each other for the crowd's entertainment in the Roman arena.[1]

1. How would you describe Telemachus's relationship with God?

_____

_____

_____

2. How did he live out his love for God?

_____

_____

_____

3. What do you think Telemachus felt when he was in the Coliseum?

_____

_____

_____

4. How did he live out his love for others?

_____

_____

_____

5. What is the message of this true story for you and me?

_____

_____

_____

Note: 1. Charles Colson, *Loving God* (Grand Rapids, Mich.: Zondervan, 1983), pp. 241-243.

 © 1996 by Gospel Light. Permission to photocopy granted.

THE LETTERS:
THE OWNER'S
MANUAL

IN THE WORD

CHECKING OUT THE OWNER'S MANUAL

The letters were written to be an encouragement and an instruction manual for living the Christian life every day. They were written to be a guidebook on issues regarding our Christian life to help us live out our faith and relationship with God every day. One of the greatest themes in the letters is that of loving God and loving others.

Loving God—Giving Yourself to God
Obedience—Read 1 John 2:3-5 and 1 John 5:2,3.

1. How do these passages define what it means to love God?

2. If we love God, why won't His commandments seem burdensome?

3. Where does following God's commandments fall for you?

Burdensome   Joyful
1   2   3   4   5   6   7   8   9   10

4. How does our obedience to God's commandments show our love for Him?

Holiness—Read 1 Peter 1:13-16

1. What does it mean to be holy as God is holy?

2. In what areas do we need to live more holy lives?

© 1996 by Gospel Light. Permission to photocopy granted.

3. How does living a life of holiness express our love for God?

....

....

....

4. What are we called to do in 1 John 2:6?

....

....

....

   What does that mean?

....

....

....

5. What are some of the ways we can walk as Jesus did?

....

....

....

Loving Others—Giving Yourself to Others

1. In Romans 13:8-10, in what area do we have a debt to one another?

....

....

....

2. What can you do to "love your neighbor as yourself"?

....

....

....

3. In Philippians 2:4, we are called to "look out for the interests of others." What keeps us from living out this verse?

....

....

....

 © 1996 by Gospel Light. Permission to photocopy granted.

4. Read James 2:15-17 and 1 John 3:16-18. What do these passages say about loving others?

....

....

....

What keeps us from doing that?

....

....

....

5. What are some practical ways we can put our love for others into action?

....

....

So What?

1. In what areas do you need to obey God more?

....

....

....

What will you do to give yourself more to God?

....

....

....

2. In what areas of your life do you need to strive to be more holy?

....

....

....

What choices do you need to make?

....

....

....

How can this group help?

....

....

....

3. Who is someone right now in your life that needs your love?

....

....

....

What will you do to show love to that person?

....

....

....

 © 1996 by Gospel Light. Permission to photocopy granted.

THINGS TO THINK ABOUT

1. What are some things that come between us and our love for God?

_____

_____

_____

2. Why do God's commands seem burdensome?

_____

_____

_____

3. In what ways has God demonstrated His love for you?

_____

_____

_____

4. What are some things that keep you from putting your love into action?

_____

_____

_____

PARENT PAGE

FAMILY ART

Everyone loves getting mail. There's something about getting a letter addressed to you. Some of the most exciting and memorable parts of the New Testament are the letters. The letters were meant to be an instruction guide for Christians on how to love God and others. Throughout the pages of the letters of the New Testament, we see encouragement and practical helps in expressing our love for God and our love to others.

Individually, take some time and draw two pictures. In the first picture, without using any words, draw a picture of what it means to love God. In the second picture, without using any words, draw a picture of what it means to love others. After you have drawn your two pictures, get back together as a family and discuss your drawings.

> Jesus replied, "'Love the Lord your God with all your heart and with all your soul and with all your mind.' This is the first and greatest commandment. And the second is like it: 'Love your neighbor as yourself.' All the Law and the Prophets hang on these two commandments" (Matthew 22:37-40).

1. What are some ways that we express our love to God as a family?

2. What are some ways that we express our love for each other and others outside our family?

3. What are some ways that we can express our love to God more as a family?

4. What are some ways that we can express our love for each other more?

How about others outside our family?

Session 11: "The Letters: The Owner's Manual" Date

 © 1996 by Gospel Light. Permission to photocopy granted.

REVELATION:
THE HOPE, ENCOURAGEMENT AND CALL

KEY VERSE

"Blessed is the one who reads the words of this prophecy, and blessed are those who hear it and take to heart what is written in it, because the time is near." Revelation 1:3

BIBLICAL BASIS

Mark 13:35-37;
1 Corinthians 13:12;
1 Thessalonians 5:4-6;
Hebrews 10:24,25;
2 Peter 3:11,12;
1 John 3:2,3;
Revelation 1:3,8; 2—3; 4:1-8;
  21:1-7; 22:7,12,20

THE BIG IDEA

Through the pages of the book of Revelation, God is calling Christians to be encouraged and to be ready for His return.

AIMS OF THIS SESSION

During this session, you will guide students to:

• Examine the book of Revelation;
• Discover the hope and the call for all Christians as the end of this age draws near;
• Implement a choice to live a life prepared for the return of Christ.

WARM UP

A LOOK AT THE END OF THE BOOK—
Students view an interpretation of the end of the world.

TEAM EFFORT— JUNIOR HIGH/ MIDDLE SCHOOL

WHAT WOULD YOU SAY?—
A discussion about how to encourage a friend who has lost hope in the imminent return of Christ.

TEAM EFFORT— HIGH SCHOOL

TIME IS TICKING—
Students discuss what they would do if they knew when Christ would return.

IN THE WORD

THE CALL OF CHRIST—
A Bible study on the call to readiness for and the encouragement of the Second Coming in the life of believers.

THINGS TO THINK ABOUT (OPTIONAL)

Questions to get students thinking and talking about their reactions to the book of Revelation.

PARENT PAGE

A tool to get the session into the home and allow parents and young people to discuss the impact of the revelations to the seven churches on their family.

REVELATION:
THE HOPE,
ENCOURAGEMENT
AND CALL

LEADER'S DEVOTIONAL

"'I am the Alpha and the Omega,' says the Lord God, 'who is, and who was, and who is to come, the Almighty'" (Revelation 1:8).

I heard a radio disk jockey recently talking about a movie currently showing in the theaters. He said he left the movie early so it ended the way he wanted it to end, rather than allow the end to be selected by the director. What an interesting way to watch movies. In reference to this popular movie he said, "Like this movie, why would I want to stick around and see the guy die?" So much for the person listening to the show who had yet to see the movie: The plot is now ruined!

Would you go ahead and watch the movie knowing the end? How about watching a game or reading a novel after discovering the final outcome? In a game, the thrill of the sport is diminished if you know your favorite team loses. Why cheer for a lost cause?

On the other hand, how would your life be different if you knew your side would win in the end? How would this reality impact your sense of hope? What encouragement would fill your heart if you thought to yourself "We're going to make it. Don't worry." Would you respond to a call from the coach of a team that is guaranteed to win? If only life would be so predictable.

The Revelation to John is filled with unique images in a distinct literary form. Interpretation varies within different sects of Christianity, but the overall purpose statement is clear. Christ will return and God's people will enter an eternal life of glory in His presence. God is what He was from the beginning, the Alpha—the First—and He is what He will be in the end, the Omega—the Last. Not only is God steadfast in His holiness throughout history, He is Almighty. He is both perfectly pure and all-powerful.

Here's the good news for us believers: God wins in the end! Christ returns and believers are drawn to Him for eternity. We are called to live in Him now with the hopeful encouragement of someday spending forever with Him. That makes living each day by faith an inviting prospect. (Written by Doug Webster)

"Yes, God's story ends 'and they lived happily ever after.'"
—Henrietta Mears

REVELATION: THE HOPE, ENCOURAGEMENT AND CALL

KEY VERSE

"Blessed is the one who reads the words of this prophecy, and blessed are those who hear it and take to heart what is written in it, because the time is near." Revelation 1:3

BIBLICAL BASIS

Mark 13:35-37; 1 Corinthians 13:12; 1 Thessalonians 5:4-6; Hebrews 10:24,25; 2 Peter 3:11,12; 1 John 3:2-3; Revelation 1:3,8; 2—3; 4:1-8; 21:1-7; 22:7,12,20

THE BIG IDEA

Through the pages of the book of Revelation, God is calling Christians to be encouraged and to be ready for His return.

WARM UP (5-10 MINUTES)

A LOOK AT THE END OF THE BOOK

• Rent the movie "Raiders of the Lost Ark" and cue up the final scene where the Ark of the Covenant is opened.
• Explain that what the group is about to see is what a lot of people think about when it comes to the end of the world. Show the scene from "Raiders of the Lost Ark".
• Ask the following questions:

1. When you think about the end of the world, what do you think of?
2. When you think of the book of Revelation what comes to mind?

---- Fold ----

1 Thessalonians 5:4-6

2 Peter 3:11,12

Revelation 3:1-3

Revelation 22:7,12,20

2. What does it mean to not be caught sleeping?

3. What are some things that distract us from being alert?

4. What can we do to stay awake, keep watch and be alert?

SO WHAT?
1. How will your life be different because of the hope in the book of Revelation?

2. In what areas do you need to be more alert?

3. How will you change your life to be more ready and alert for His return?

Take a minute and write a note to God expressing your thanks for the encouragement He gives and to prepare your heart to be ready for His return.
Dear God,

Love Always,

THINGS TO THINK ABOUT (OPTIONAL)

• Use the questions on page 168 after or as a part of "In the Word."
1. When you think of Revelation or the end of the world, what comes to mind?
2. How does what we discussed today impact your attitude toward your non-Christian friends and family members?
3. What is the greatest hope or encouragement that you have heard in this lesson?
4. Read Hebrews 10:24,25. What are some things we can do to encourage each other as we see the day approaching?

PARENT PAGE

• Distribute page to parents.

TEAM EFFORT—JUNIOR HIGH/MIDDLE SCHOOL (15-20 Minutes)

WHAT WOULD YOU SAY?

- Give each student a copy of "What Would You Say?" on page 163, or display a copy on an overhead projector.
- Read and discuss the case study and the questions that follow.
- Option: Divide students into pairs and have them develop a role-play about what they would say to Michelle. If there is time, have them share the role-play before the whole group.

You have been friends with Michelle for a long time. Your families have been friends since you were in grade school. The two of you have spent a lot of time together, hanging out, having fun and talking about life and God. Both of you share a special bond. There is nothing you could not say to each other.

Yet over the past few months you've seen a change in Michelle. She's not as concerned about church, the Christian life or anything else to do with God. You're concerned because she was the one who really encouraged you in your walk with God when you became a Christian. She was a role model for you in what being a Christian was all about. Now what you see in her life is something different.

Over the last month, you've been hearing rumors about Michelle. She's been hanging out with a new set of friends whose lives are very different from the Michelle you used to know. She has stopped going to church, and has begun pulling away from the friends she used to hang out with, including you. You have decided to talk with her.

Over a Coke and a large order of fries, you bring up the issue. You tell her that you've been concerned about her for a few months now. You tell her that she seems to have changed. As you bring up the issue of God in her life, she cuts you off and says, "I'm just tired of being a Christian. I just want to do my own thing for a while. Besides, I can always change later and get serious again about a relationship with God."

What would you say to her?

1. Why do you think Michelle's attitude has changed?
2. Why do many people have Michelle's attitude?
3. What does it mean to be ready for the return of Christ?
4. How does someone prepare for the return of Christ?

TEAM EFFORT—HIGH SCHOOL (15-20 Minutes)

TIME IS TICKING

- Divide students into groups of four or five.
- Give each group a set of 3x5-inch cards on which you have written the following:

Card One   1 hour   Card Four   1 year
Card Two   1 week   Card Five   10 years
Card Three   1 month

- Distribute a card to each member of each group without anyone seeing each other's cards.
Ask the groups the following question:
How would you feel and what would you do if the world were going to end in the time listed on your card?
- After giving the groups time to share their reactions, bring the whole group together and have a few people share their reactions.
- Discuss the following questions:

1. What were your feelings and reactions to the time given you?
2. How would your life be different because of your time frame?

3. What happened to your group members' reactions as the time got shorter and shorter?
4. What are some lessons that can be applied to our lives today?

IN THE WORD (25-30 Minutes)

THE CALL OF CHRIST

- Divide students into groups of three or four.
- Give each student a copy of "The Call of Christ" on pages 164-167 and a pen or pencil, or display a copy on an overhead projector.
- Have students complete the Bible study.

The book of Revelation is a book of hope, encouragement, judgment and a call to all Christians. Within the pages, we see the scenes of the end of the world, the triumph of God over Satan, the final judgment of the world and the incredible description of what heaven will be like. Through the pages of Revelation, God is calling His believers to stand firm, be encouraged and be ready for the return of Christ.

BE ENCOURAGED

1. What hope or promise is found in the following passages?

1 Corinthians 13:12
....
1 John 3:1,2
....
Revelation 21:1-7
....

2. Read Revelation 4:1-8. What would it be like to see God face-to-face?
....
What would you say to Him?
....

3. What does it mean to know Him even as He knows us?
....

4. As you read Revelation 21:1-7, which words best describe your feelings?

Thankful	Valuable	Relieved	Awe-filled
Renewed	Unworthy	Amazed	Complete

5. How do these promises affect your life right now?
....

BE READY

1. What encouragement are we given in the following passages?

Mark 13:35-37
....

Fold

TEAM EFFORT

WHAT WOULD YOU SAY?

You have been friends with Michelle for a long time. Your families have been friends since you were in grade school. The two of you have spent a lot of time together, hanging out, having fun and talking about life and God. Both of you share a special bond. There is nothing you could not say to each other.

Yet over the past few months you've seen a change in Michelle. She's not as concerned about church, the Christian life or anything else to do with God. You're concerned because she was the one who really encouraged you in your walk with God when you became a Christian. She was a role model for you in what being a Christian was all about. Now what you see in her life is something different.

Over the last month, you've been hearing rumors about Michelle. She's been hanging out with a new set of friends whose lives are very different from the Michelle you used to know. She has stopped going to church, and has begun pulling away from the friends she used to hang out with, including you. You have decided to talk with her.

Over a Coke and a large order of fries, you bring up the issue. You tell her that you've been concerned about her for a few months now. You tell her that she seems to have changed. As you bring up the issue of God in her life, she cuts you off and says, "I'm just tired of being a Christian. I just want to do my own thing for a while. Besides, I can always change later and get serious again about a relationship with God."

What would you say to her?

1. Why do you think Michelle's attitude has changed?

_____

_____

_____

2. Why do many people have Michelle's attitude?

_____

_____

_____

3. What does it mean to be ready for the return of Christ?

_____

_____

_____

4. How does someone prepare for the return of Christ?

_____

_____

_____

 © 1996 by Gospel Light. Permission to photocopy granted.

REVELATION:
THE HOPE,
ENCOURAGEMENT
AND CALL

IN THE WORD

THE CALL OF CHRIST

The book of Revelation is a book of hope, encouragement, judgment and a call to all Christians. Within the pages, we see the scenes of the end of the world, the triumph of God over Satan, the final judgment of the world and the incredible description of what heaven will be like. Through the pages of Revelation, God is calling His believers to stand firm, be encouraged and be ready for the return of Christ.

Be Encouraged

1. What hope or promise is found in the following passages?

   1 Corinthians 13:12

   _____
   _____
   _____

   1 John 3:2,3

   _____
   _____
   _____

   Revelation 21:1-7

   _____
   _____
   _____

2. Read Revelation 4:1-8. What would it be like to see God face-to-face?

   _____
   _____
   _____

   What would you say to Him?

   _____
   _____
   _____

© 1996 by Gospel Light. Permission to photocopy granted.

3. What does it mean to know Him even as He knows us?

....

....

....

4. As you read Revelation 21:1-7, which word best describes your feeling?

Thankful	Relieved
Valuable	Awe-filled
Renewed	Amazed
Unworthy	Complete

5. How do those promises affect your life in the here and now?

....

....

....

Be Ready

1. What encouragement are we given in the following passages?

Mark 13:35-37

....

....

....

1 Thessalonians 5:4-6

....

....

....

2 Peter 3:11,12

....

....

....

 © 1996 by Gospel Light. Permission to photocopy granted.

REVELATION:
THE HOPE,
ENCOURAGEMENT
AND CALL

Revelation 3:1-3

Revelation 22:7,12,20

2. What does it mean to not be caught sleeping?

3. What are some things that distract us from being alert?

4. What can we do to stay awake, keep watch and be alert?

So What?

1. How will your life be different because of the hope of the book of Revelation?

2. In what areas do you need to be more alert?

© 1996 by Gospel Light. Permission to photocopy granted.

3. How will you change your life to be more ready and alert for His return?

....

....

....

....

....

....

Take a minute and write a note to God expressing your thanks for the encouragement He gives and to prepare your heart to be ready for His return.

Dear God,

....

....

....

....

....

....

Love Always,

....

 © 1996 by Gospel Light. Permission to photocopy granted.

THINGS TO THINK ABOUT

1. When you think of Revelation or the end of the world, what comes to mind?

....

....

....

2. How does what we discussed today impact your attitude toward your non-Christian friends and family members?

....

....

....

3. What is the greatest hope or encouragement that you have heard in this lesson?

....

....

....

4. Read Hebrews 10:24,25. What are some things we can do to encourage each other as we see the day approaching?

....

....

....

© 1996 by Gospel Light. Permission to photocopy granted.

PARENT PAGE

THEN AND NOW

The book of Revelation is a book of hope. Within the pages it offers the hope to each Christian that even though life may be difficult, the battle is already won. It offers the hope that someday we will be with Him in heaven in the newness of a transformed life, yet the book of Revelation has another message—one of readiness and encouragement.

Read the following letters to the seven churches listed in Revelation 2—3. Write down what the message was for each church, and then apply the message to your family.

The Church in Ephesus (Revelation 2:1-7)
Then: ....
Now: ....

The Church in Smyrna (Revelation 2:8-11)
Then: ....
Now: ....

The Church in Pergamum (Revelation 2:12-17)
Then: ....
Now: ....

The Church in Thyatira (Revelation 2:18-29)
Then: ....
Now: ....

The Church in Sardis (Revelation 3:1-6)
Then: ....
Now: ....

The Church in Philadelphia (Revelation 3:7-13)
Then: ....
Now: ....

The Church in Laodicea (Revelation 3:14-22)
Then: ....
Now: ....

1. Which message to a church is closest to home for your family right now?

....
....
....

 © 1996 by Gospel Light. Permission to photocopy granted.

2. What do you need to do about that message as a family?

....
....
....

3. What three action steps will you take as a family to work on that area?

Action Step One:

....
....
....

Action Step Two:

....
....
....

Action Step Three:

....
....
....

Session 12: "Revelation: The Hope,
Encouragement and Call"
Date ....

© 1996 by Gospel Light. Permission to photocopy granted.

Add a New Member to Your Youth Staff.

Jim Burns is president of the National Institute of Youth Ministry.

Meet Jim Burns. He won't play guitar and he doesn't do windows, but he will take care of your programming needs. That's because his new curriculum, **YouthBuilders Group Bible Studies**, is a comprehensive program designed to take your group through their high school years. (If you have junior high kids in your group, **YouthBuilders** works for them too.)

For less than $6 a month, you'll get Jim Burns' special recipe of high-involvement, discussion-oriented, Bible-centered studies. It's the next generation of Bible curriculum for youth—and with Jim on your staff, you'll be free to spend more time one-on-one with the kids in your group.

Here are some of Youth-Builders' hottest features:

- Reproducible pages—one book fits your whole group
- Wide appeal—big groups, small groups—even adjusts to combine junior high/high school groups
- Hits home—special section to involve parents with every session of the study
- Interactive Bible discovery—geared to help young people find answers themselves
- Cheat sheets—a Bible *Tuck-In*™ with all the session information on a single page
- Flexible format—perfect for Sunday mornings, midweek youth meetings, or camps and retreats
- Three studies in one—each study has three four-session modules that examine critical life choices.

     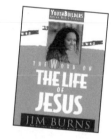

12 Books in the Series!

The Word on Sex, Drugs & Rock 'N' Roll
ISBN 08307.16424 $16.99

The Word on Prayer and the Devotional Life
ISBN 08307.16432 $16.99

The Word on the Basics of Christianity
ISBN 08307.16440 $16.99

The Word on Being a Leader, Serving Others & Sharing Your Faith
ISBN 08307.16459 $16.99

The Word on Helping Friends in Crisis
ISBN 08307.16467 $16.99

The Word on the Life of Jesus
ISBN 08307.16475 $16.99

The Word on Finding and Using Your Spiritual Gifts
ISBN 08307.17897 $16.99

The Word on the Sermon on the Mount
ISBN 08307.17234 $16.99

The Word on Spiritual Warfare
ISBN 08307.17242 $16.99

The Word on the New Testament
ISBN 08307.17250 $16.99

The Word on the Old Testament
ISBN 08307.17269 $16.99

The Word on Family
ISBN 08307.17277 $16.99

More Great Resources from Jim Burns

Drugproof Your Kids
Stephen Arterburn and Jim Burns

Solid biblical principles are combined with the most effective prevention and intervention techniques to give parents a guide they can trust.
ISBN 08307.17714 $10.99

Drugproof Your Kids Video

A 90-minute seminar featuring Stephen Arterburn and Jim Burns. Includes a reproducible syllabus.
SPCN 85116.00876 $19.99

Parenting Teens Positively
Video *Featuring Jim Burns*

Understand the forces shaping the world of a teenager and what you can do to be a positive influence. This powerful message of hope is for anyone working with—or living with—youth. Includes reproducible syllabus. UPC 607135.000655 $29.99

Surviving Adolescence
Jim Burns

Jim Burns helps teens—and their parents—negotiate the path from adolescence to adulthood with real-life stories that show how to make it through the teen years in one piece. ISBN 08307.20650 $9.99

For these and more great resources and to learn about NIYM's leadership training, call **1-800-397-9725.**

Gospel Light

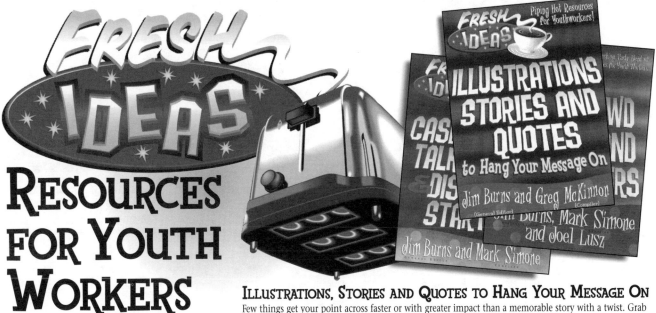

FRESH IDEAS

RESOURCES FOR YOUTH WORKERS

Jim Burns, General Editor

Turn your youth group meetings into dynamic, exciting events that kids look forward to attending week after week! Supercharge your messages, grab their attention with your activities and connect with kids the first time and every time with these great resources. Just try to keep these books on the shelf!

ILLUSTRATIONS, STORIES AND QUOTES TO HANG YOUR MESSAGE ON

Few things get your point across faster or with greater impact than a memorable story with a twist. Grab your teens' attention by talking with your mouth full of unforgettable stories.
Manual, ISBN 08307.18834 **$16.99**

CASE STUDIES, TALK SHEETS AND DISCUSSION STARTERS

Teens learn best when they talk—not when you talk at them. A discussion allowing youth to discover the truth for themselves, with your guidance, is a powerful experience that will stay with them for a lifetime.
Manual, ISBN 08307.18842 **$16.99**

GAMES, CROWDBREAKERS AND COMMUNITY BUILDERS

Dozens of innovative, youth-group-tested ideas for fun and original crowdbreakers, as well as successful plans and trips for building a sense of community in your group.
Manual, ISBN 08307.18818 **$16.99**

More Resources for Youth Workers, Parents & Students

Steering Them Straight
Stephen Arterburn & Jim Burns

Parents can find understanding as well as practical tools to deal with crisis situations. Includes guidelines that will help any family prevent problems before they develop.
UPC 156179.4066 **$10.99**

The Youth Builder
Jim Burns

This Gold Medallion Award winner provides you with proven methods, specific recommendations and hands-on examples of handling and understanding the problems and challenges of youth ministry.
ISBN 089081.1576. **$16.95**

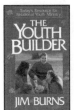

Spirit Wings
Jim Burns

In the language of today's teens, these 84 short devotionals will encourage youth to build a stronger and more intimate relationship with God.
ISBN 08928.37837 **$10.95**

Radical Love
Book & Video, Jim Burns

In *Radical Love* kids discover why it's best to wait on God's timing, how to say no when their bodies say yes and how to find forgiveness for past mistakes.
Paperback, ISBN 08307.17935 **$9.99**
VHS Video, SPCN 85116.00922 **$19.99**

90 Days Through the New Testament
Jim Burns

A growth experience through the New Testament that lays the foundation for developing a daily time with God.
ISBN 08307.14561 **$9.99**

Getting in Touch with God
Jim Burns

Develop a consistent and disciplined time with God in the midst of hectic schedules as Jim Burns shares with you inspiring devotional readings to deepen your love of God.
ISBN 08908.15208 **$2.95**

Radical Christianity
Book & Video, Jim Burns

Radical Christianity is a proven plan to help youth live a life that's worth living and make a difference in their world.
Paperback, ISBN 08307.17927 **$9.99**
VHS Video, SPCN 85116.01082 **$19.99**

The Youth Worker's Book of Case Studies
Jim Burns

Fifty-two true stories with discussion questions to add interest to Bible studies.
ISBN 08307.15827 **$12.99**

To order NIYM resources, please call
1-800-397-9725
or to learn how you can take advantage of NIYM training opportunities call or write to:
NIYM • PO Box 297 • San Juan Capistrano
CA 92675 • 949/487-0217

What in the world is *NIYM*?

A.) The Neurotically Inclined Yo-Yo Masters
B.) The Neatest Incidental Yearbook Mystery
C.) The Natural Ignition Yields of Marshmallows
D.) The National Institute of Youth Ministry

If you deliberately picked A, B, or C you're the reason Jim Burns started NIYM! If you picked D, you can go to the next page. In any case, you could learn more about NIYM. Here are some IQ score-raisers:

Jim Burns started NIYM to:
• Meet the growing needs of training and equipping youth workers and parents
• Develop excellent resources and events for young people—in the U.S. and internationally
• Empower young people and their families to make wise decisions and experience a vital Christian lifestyle.

NIYM can make a difference in your life and enhance your youth work skills through these special events:

Institutes—These consist of week-long, in-depth small-group training sessions for youth workers.

Trainer of Trainees—NIYM will train you to train others. You can use this training with your volunteers, parents and denominational events. You can go through the certification process and become an official NIYM associate. (No, you don't get a badge or decoder ring).

International Training—Join NIYM associates to bring youth ministry to kids and adults around the world. (You'll learn meanings to universal words like "yo!" and "hey!')

Custom Training—These are special training events for denominational groups, churches, networks, colleges and seminaries.

Parent Forums—We'll come to your church or community with two incredible hours of learning, interaction and fellowship. It'll be fun finding out who makes your kids tick!

Youth Events—Dynamic speakers, interaction and drama bring a powerful message to kids through a fun and fast-paced day. Our youth events include: This Side Up, Radical Respect, Surviving Adolescence and Peer Leadership.

For brain food or a free information packet about the National Institute of Youth Ministry, write to:

NIYM
P.O. Box 297 • San Juan Capistrano, CA 92675
Tel: (949) 487-0217 • Fax: (949) 487-1758 • Info@niym.org